To Borra

Best wishes

Chris

Writing Soap

Aber Creative Writing Guides

Aber publishing

Writing Soap

How to write
popular continuing drama

Chris Thompson

www.aber-publishing.co.uk

Disclaimer

The information given in this book is given in good faith but the television industry is one that is subject to rapid change. Neither the author nor the publisher nor all/any of their agents can be held responsible for outcomes that result from actions taken due to the information in this book. Readers are advised to take appropriate professional advice before entering into agreements with third parties.

With thanks to MV Studios Limited for permission to use copyright material included in this book.

Author Note

In this text we have included examples from actual Emmerdale scripts. In a television production these scripts are actually written on the right hand side of the page only. This allows the actors and directors to annotate the scripts. However if we had set them out in this manner, you would have a book with blank half pages, hence we have typeset them, quite deliberately, in this manner.

This edition published in 2011 by Aber Publishing, P.O. Box 225, Abergele, LL18 9AY, United Kingdom
Aber Publishing is a division of GLMP Ltd.

ISBN: 978-1-84285-118-0

Website: http://www.aber-publishing.co.uk

Typeset by Vikatan Publishing Solutions, Chennai, India
Printed and bound in TK

Contents

Story-Beats and *Beats*

These are two terms that often cause new writers a great deal of difficulty and it is quite easy to see why. We regularly talk about story beats but they are not the same as (BEAT) the stage direction. A story beat is actually an individual story point.

When we are giving Stage Direction, the term we use is (BEAT) which is often inserted in the middle of a speech. It is a mini—pause, a single heart-beat, or breathing space, if you like. It can be used where a character is having difficulty saying something, struggling with their emotions, or it can allow them to change tack.

Foreword

'Chris Thompson is a master of his art and this book offers a very rare opportunity to share in his knowledge, experience and insight. It is a clear, concise yet highly detailed guide to the dense, seemingly impenetrable and often unforgiving world of Soap writing. It will prove invaluable both to aspiring writers embarking on their first script and to established writers wishing to hone their skills in the company of one of Soap's most prolific and successful contributors. In short, if you have any ambition to write Soap scripts (or write better Soap scripts) before you do anything else, read this book!'

Steve November
Executive Producer

Emmerdale
Yorkshire Television

Introduction

The reasoning behind this book

'Soap Operas' have been a vital part of the landscape of British, and indeed international, television for many years. *Coronation Street* started life in 1960, *Emmerdale* in 1972, *Eastenders* in 1985, while relative newcomers *Hollyoaks* and *Doctors*, began in 1995 and 2000 respectively. They deliver huge ratings, generate vast income and are held dear by millions of people, week in and week out.

But far more important to the Television writer, they provide regular income; offer the opportunity to have your work seen by a huge audience, and open doors to other areas of television drama and film. Most of the Soaps have a team of twenty or more scriptwriters, some with years of experience, and others who are new to the job. And in an age when it is becoming more and more difficult to have individually authored work commissioned, it is an option would-be TV writers can ill afford to ignore.

This book aims to provide you with an understanding of how these programmes are made; but more important, it seeks to give you practical skills, supported by a series of exercises, which will give you the tools to enable you to do the job. It contains expert advice from someone who has been writing professionally since 1985, with almost five hundred TV and Radio credits, among them, over 200 episodes of ITV's *Emmerdale* and 150 episodes of the BBC Radio 4 Drama, *The Archers*.

Chris Thompson
chris.thompson@aber-publishing.co.uk

1

A step-by-step approach

When you watch an episode of a Soap, you are seeing the result of a complex, demanding and rigorous process, which began months (or even years) before, when the germ of an idea was raised at a story conference or delivered by an individual writer. It can take several months to bring a story to screen, and may take up to two or three years to play out.

It might sometimes look easy, but it isn't. The pressures are enormous, to deliver quality scripts on time, to a high standard, to function as a team member, coming up with new stories and sharing in the collective responsibility of keeping the show fresh and appealing. And, above all, making sure the audiences remain high.

Each chapter in this book will look at an aspect of Writing Soap, first of all explaining in detail the production process, before concentrating on specific writing skills that can be learned and put into practice.

The first part of the book looks at GETTING IN. It helps you to learn the skills to write the scripts and offers practical advice on how to approach one of the major Soaps, and to persuade them to give you a job.

The second part looks at ways of STAYING IN. It's one thing to be given the chance to write for Soap, but plenty of writers who are given that chance, fall within the first few months. They find it hard to deliver on their initial promise, become fazed by the pressure and the demands of delivering quality scripts on time, involving several drafts and find themselves receiving the dread phone call telling them their services are no longer required.

What this book can and can't do

It can show you how the programmes are made. It can show you the skills to do the job. It can give you helpful tips on how to get in and sustain a career.

What it can't do is guarantee you a job. Nor can it give you the innate ability to write for Soap. Many good writers find the process too constricting and too inhibiting. They are either unable or unwilling to suppress their own individuality as writers, writing for characters they didn't invent, telling stories they didn't pitch and may not feel sympathy for. They feel affronted by the editing process, which will on occasions ask them to make fundamental changes to their work.

You will need qualities that are beyond the remit of this or any other book. You will need determination, self-belief, perseverance, the ability to take criticism, to turn a script round in days, to come up with a new scene in a matter of hours when an actor falls ill, for example, or bad weather means an exterior scene has to be re-located to Studio. A Soap is not a movie, which may run over time and over budget. The schedules are unrelenting and the machine has to keep rolling on.

The book can't tell you how to deal with the insecurity of being a writer. Apart from *Coronation Street*, Soaps rarely offer extended contracts to writers: you are commissioned on a script-by-script basis, and if the producer decides your time is up, that's it, no severance pay, just the staggered payments from work already in the system (fees are usually paid in three or four stages: signature, delivery, acceptance and repeat, if you're lucky). I came from what is regarded as a very stable profession, teaching. I was Deputy Head in a large comprehensive when I took the plunge, giving up the security of the job, holidays and pension and entering one of the most insecure professions in the world. And it wasn't just me: my wife and I had two young children and I was the main breadwinner. Do I have any regrets? None …

And while I'm letting you know what you're in for, let me dispel a couple of myths. People often ask me if I write for particular characters or write particular storylines. The answer is an emphatic no, in both cases. If you work on Soap, you are commissioned to write whole scripts, with whatever characters and stories are to be told in that half hour.

People are often confused about how continuity is sustained and ask "do you pick up from where the last person left off …" Of course, as you will see later, the process is far more structured than that, with many checks and balances along the way.

But enough of the things the book can't do. As well as giving you practical advice, I hope the book will convey the thrill and the satisfaction of entertaining millions of people every week. It is quite a responsibility, but one that has given me a fulfilling and rewarding life. Surely there is nothing better than doing the thing you love and being well paid for it? As you are reading this book, I guess you agree with me.

Are the opportunities real?

I wouldn't be writing this book, if I didn't believe that some of you, who read it, have the chance to become successful writers of Soap. When I joined the *Emmerdale* team, in 1998, I was already an established writer on both Radio and Television. But many of the writers I have worked alongside subsequently got their first TV breakthrough writing for the show. So, it is both a way in to writing for television, and an option available to established writers.

Some move on to other things, some fall by the wayside, but go on to work on other programmes. For others it may be the only TV work they ever do, but they have the satisfaction of having fulfilled a dream and it can lead to career opportunities outside the TV industry.

But as long as there are successful long running series, there will be a need for writers, to refresh and renew the programmes and to move them on. When I was commissioned to write my first radio play in 1985, I thanked, effusively, the Producer who had placed his faith in me and my work. He replied by thanking me, saying that without me and others like me, he wouldn't have a job. Without writers, there would be no Soap, nor any other TV drama. Someone has to do it: why not you?

A task
How much do you know?
If you have watched Soap over the years, jot down the following:

Which Soap have you enjoyed and watched the most, and why? What makes it appealing to you?

Which episodes stand out as being especially memorable?
What made them stick in your memory: was it a
spectacular stunt, a moment of heightened emotional
drama or something more low key but truthful?
Finally, if you don't watch Soap, START NOW ...

Part I
Getting in

1   I can do that

An overview

This chapter will tell you about the distinctive nature of writing Soap. It will tell you what sets it apart from writing for the stage, say, or having your own authored work produced on Radio or Television. It will explain the way in which the programmes are made, letting you know who does what, and highlighting the role of the script writer.

But first a little test.

How much do you really know about Soap?

A common cry when watching an episode of Soap, is "I can do that". It can look so easy, especially as many of the characters are recognisable, "ordinary" folk, speaking down to earth language, and dealing with the stuff of everyday life: falling in and out of love, bereavement, infidelity, illness, childbirth and so forth.

So, choose your favourite Soap. Think back to the last episode you watched. Ask yourself the following questions:

How many scenes were in the episode?

How many characters?

How much took place in Studio sets?

How much on location?

How many story strands did the episode contain?

What was the main story strand running through the episode?

What was the hook, or cliff hanger at the end of the episode?

You may find this hard to do from memory, but have a try. Then, watch and record another episode. Analyse it in the light of the questions above. You may be surprised by the answers. What you need to realise, is that, for the scriptwriter, those factors are the beginning of the process of writing a script. They have to work within given constraints of cast numbers, studio/location balance, story priority and so forth. There will be more on this later, but for now, bear in mind the following:

> Cast numbers are determined by the needs of the story but also by budget. It is wasteful to have a big player in an episode speaking a couple of lines, or worse, saying nothing at all.
>
> All the main Soaps have permanent Studio sets. They are cheaper to use than location, which is expensive in terms of time and money.
>
> Each episode should have an A strand story, which will give it a spine. It will also have several other stories running alongside it, at various stages of development.

How the programmes are made

As with any drama, the idea is to think of a story, write the script, film it and put it on screen. It sounds easy, but bear in mind; we are talking about series that are on our screens several times a week: *Emmerdale*, for instance, is shown over six episodes a week, which amounts to 312 episodes a year. That is a lot of story, a lot of characters and presents an immense challenge in terms of keeping an audience interested, keeping them coming back for more.

As I mentioned above, each show has a permanent studio base. This will usually contain some of the heavily used communal sets, where characters can interact across different story strands: the pubs, *The Woolpack, Rover's Return* and *Queen Vic*, naturally, but also *Roy's cafe, Underworld, the Doctors' Surgery*, as well as domestic sets for key families. From time-to-time the fixed studio sets will change: the pub may undergo a facelift for example; a house may be destroyed by fire and needs to be out of action for a while; a domestic set may become redundant, if the characters that live there leave. It costs time and money to strike a set and replace it, so these decisions are not taken lightly.

They also have fixed exterior locations: *Coronation Street* itself, behind the old Granada studios but due to rebuilt in Media City where it will move to in 2012, the village of *Emmerdale*, purpose-built in the grounds of Harewood House, near Leeds and the Square in *Eastenders*, a permanent set. Beyond that, other locations will be used as dictated by story. Most shows will base around 60% of any single episode in Studio Sets.

On *Emmerdale* and *Coronation Street*, every few weeks, the writing team meets for a Story conference. On *Emmerdale*, these take place every four weeks (on *Coronation Street* every three). These last two to three days and this is where the stories are generated. Around the table will be the Series Producer, the Story Editor, the Script Producer, the scriptwriting team, the Script Editors, the Storyline Writers, and the programme's researcher. That is over thirty people and at long term conferences (held three or four times a year to look at longer term story arcs) two or three Senior Executives turn up as well. That is the forum in which the writer is expected to pitch new stories, suggestions for new characters and to join in the hurly burly of the discussion.

Eastenders used to work differently, with a core of experienced writers and many more beyond, who were less involved in decision making. On *Doctors*, writers pitch individual stories, which play over one episode alongside ongoing strands, the personal and professional lives of the main characters. But however individual programmes work, stories have to come from somewhere, and surely one of the main reasons we become writers is because we like to tell stories.

Chapter four deals in detail with the conference and how to survive it but is the place where it all begins. And if it sounds daunting, it can also be exhilarating. Uniquely, it offers the writer, that loneliest of souls, the opportunity to work as the member of a team, with all the fun that can entail. Not everyone relishes the situation. Only you can know if it's for you. But given the chance, take it!

The purpose of the conference, On *Coronation Street* and *Emmerdale*, is to generate ideas for a block of episodes. Once the conference is over, the team of storyline writers will turn the raw material into 18 or 24 single episodes. They don't write dialogue, but produce a four of five page prose document, detailing the storyline strands that have to be carried in individual episodes. This is called *THE STORYLINE DOCUMENT.* (It's a confusing title because it contains more than one storyline). The scriptwriters are then commissioned to write these episodes and turn them into scripts, which will end up on screen, following several edits and drafts.

From receiving the commission, to the episode being screened takes approximately four months. A scriptwriter can be working on up to six scripts at any one time, at different stages of development.

Once the scripts are finished, they are delivered to the people who actually put the programme on screen: the Director, the Actors and the array of Production staff: the lighting Cameraman, Sound supervisor and people in Costume, Make-up and Props. In addition, someone will time the rehearsal scripts to ensure they run to the exact time required.

The filming schedules are tight, with several episodes being filmed over a three-week cycle. There is little of no time for rehearsal and the actors have to become as skilled as the writers in working to a high standard under extreme pressure.

Who does what?

I'm not going to outline every single task in the Production process, but as a scriptwriter, you will work closely with a number of people and need to develop effective working relationships with them.

The series producer

This is the person responsible for the day to day running of the show and the person who will offer you a place on the writing team, if he or she likes your work. It is an enormously stressful job and the average tenure is about two to four years. During that time, the Series Producer will want to make his or her mark, setting the tone, chairing the conferences and making all the key decisions about story and casting and the direction of the show. They will also want the shows to make headlines, to make the front covers of the many magazines which feature the world of popular drama, to generate interest in the wider world and above all, to increase the audience.

The executive producer

This is the person at a level above the series producer. He or she will probably have oversight of several programmes. They will leave the day to day running of the show to the series producer but will provide support and a critical eye when necessary. They will almost certainly have experience of being a series producer.

The script editors

The script editors are the people who work closely with the writers on their scripts. Each draft of a script will be read by them, by the story producer and Series Producer, and the final draft will also be read by the Director. They will each have an input into your script and their notes and ideas will be conveyed to you by the script editor. This process is discussed in greater detail in Part Two of the book.

The story editor

This is the person who runs the team of Storyline Writers and is responsible for putting out individual episodes in synopsis form. If you have a story idea it can be helpful to discuss it with the story editor before taking the plunge and pitching it round the table.

The researcher

When you write an original play or screenplay, you expect to do your own research. Soaps are always dealing with stories that require information about the law, about various illnesses and their treatment, police procedure, drug abuse and so on. It is vital that what goes on screen is accurate. If it isn't, then a programme could cause offence, especially when tacking sensitive issues, or be open to ridicule, if it gets something wrong. Programmes will therefore often employ a full time researcher, whose job is to provide the necessary information. They will build up a network of contacts and, on *Emmerdale*, produce a research document which is issued alongside the storyline documents each month.

The archivist

Programmes which have been running for twenty years or more have a long history. It is important to understand that history and to be aware of long standing relationships between various characters. The archivist can provide that information, look up past episodes for reference and make sure that what goes out in scripts in the present accurately reflects the past.

The scriptwriter

Your degree of involvement in planning the future of the shows and coming up with stories will vary from programme to programme. Some Soaps take pride in being writer-led and you will be expected to have an input into the story process. It would seem foolish, therefore not take that opportunity. Better to have your say than to sit back and moan about the stories you have to tell.

Most important, however, you will be expected to turn the storyline document into a lively, original piece of drama, putting your own stamp on the material, while remaining within the voice and remit of the show. Good Soap writers have their own style and their individuality can shine through. I shall say much more later on in the book about how to do this.

A footnote

You'll have realised by now that audience figures play an enormous part in writing for popular drama. An audience slump can lead to jobs being lost, or, in some cases, shows being scrapped. This is what happened to *Brookside*, whose audience fell to less than one million, and stayed there, leading to its demise.

Audiences are gauged in two ways. The number of viewers and audience share. In the days of four channels, Soaps could gather upwards of 20 million viewers. In the multi-channel climate of today, the figures are more likely to be between 6 and 10 million. It's still an awful lot of people, but executives are just as concerned, if not more so, about audience share. That is, what percentage of people watching TV at the time a Soap is on, are watching that Soap. Years ago it would have been over 50%, now it's more likely to be between 30% and 40%, still impressive when viewers have so much choice in terms of channels and other forms of home-based entertainment. The numbers are studied avidly, and Producers will have "overnights" on their computers the morning after an episode has gone out, which will give them a rough idea of how many people were watching.

Before we move on, another test:

Test your understanding

Think of a story that has been screened in your favourite Soap. Ask yourself the following questions:

How long did the story run for?
Who were the main protagonists in the story?
What repercussions did the story have on other characters in the show?
Did the story have surprising twists and turns?
What were the key moments in the telling of the story?
What made the story successful/unsuccessful in your opinion?
Was it comic, tragic, melodramatic, or a mixture of all four?
Was it led by a character, or based around an issue?

You should realise that different stories have different length, weight and impact. Some may run for a few weeks, others may have repercussion lasting for years. All successful Soaps will combine those different types of story, but each must be told with freshness, surprise and boldness.

You should by now understand the way the Soap operates and is made. Time to move on …

2   **If only you'll let me in ...**

An overview

Getting a job writing for television isn't easy, but you have more chance of being accepted on Soap than of having an original piece commissioned. Indeed, the BBC's daytime Soap, *Doctors*, has in the past set out to find writers new to television and to give them a break. Some have gone on to work on programmes like the BBC's *Casualty* and *Holby City*, or moved to another prime-time Soap. This chapter tells you how to maximise your chances and to avoid making mistakes that will waste your time and that of your prospective employers.

In an ideal world

... you would have already have had work published or broadcast. You would have an agent, who would contact the programme on your behalf. You would then wait and see if the offer came in.

However, I imagine that you are probably not in that situation, but never fear, plenty of writers have trodden the self-same path and ended up with long and successful careers.

Write

This may be stating the obvious, but when you contact a Producer, they will want to read something you have written. It should preferably be Drama, and could be a film script, TV script, stage play or Radio play. It doesn't have to have been published or broadcast, but the Producer needs to know if you can write, if your work can leap off the page and persuade them that you may have something to offer their programme.

You should get in touch first, by letter or email; giving a brief CV and asking if you can send some work for them to consider. If you are approaching a Soap, **DON'T** send in an imaginary episode of that programme. If the Producer likes your work, he or she will ask you to do a trial script of their show. It will probably be an episode that has already been written by one of the writing team. That is the point at which they will decide if you can fit your particular style to the demands of the show.

The first piece of work you send will be your *Calling Card* script. Before I got into TV writing, I had had several Radio plays broadcast, so that body of work was my calling card. However, I then had to prove I could adapt and write for television.

You may already have a number of scripts ready to send but if not, you would be advised to read Steve Wetton's excellent book **Writing TV Scripts,** in this Aber Writers Guides series. It will teach you everything you need to know about the techniques involved in writing TV drama, outside Soap Opera. A thirty or sixty minute TV script of your own choosing would be a good *Calling Card.*

You should also have watched the programme you want to work on and be able to talk about it: its strengths and weaknesses and what you could bring to the mix. If you get the opportunity to meet the Producer, who likes your work enough to invite you in, you need to show enthusiasm for and an understanding of the programme and demonstrate what you could bring to it.

Radio Drama

Don't discount Radio Drama as a way of beginning your professional career. Radio 4 broadcasts several original dramas a week and a good number of them will be by new writers. Listen to the output and try to write a 45 or 30 minute single drama. Identify a producer whose work you like and send them your script. Full time Producers are based primarily in London, Manchester, Birmingham, Glasgow, Cardiff and Belfast. Where possible, send work to the Region in which you live and work. The BBC also has a "Writers' Room" where new writers can send their work. Finally, there are a number of independent Radio companies producing drama. Details of all these potential markets can be found in *The Writers' and Artists' Yearbook,* which is published annually.

Agents

Agents can be a terrific help in getting into TV but acquiring one can be tricky. They will have a stable of established writers but will from time to time take on new writers. If you have written your *Calling Card* script, then it can do no harm to send it to an Agent, as well as to a TV producer. Again, a list of agents can be found in *The Writers' and Artists' Yearbook.* You have nothing to lose. The worst they can do is to say no.

If at first you don't succeed ...

Before I wrote my first Radio Play I had sent in several unsolicited TV scripts to various companies, all of which were rejected. My breakthrough as a Radio writer came through a competition in the Radio Times.

I applied to write for *The Archers,* three times over a period of about six years. My first two approaches got nowhere, the third one led to a very happy spell of over four years on the programme, during which I wrote 150 episodes. Each approach, incidentally, was made to a different Producer. And by the time of my third approach, I was much more experienced, with professional credits to my name.

So, if you do get rejected, don't give in, try another programme, start another script, contact another agent.

A summary

If you are serious about being a professional writer, then make writing a part of your life. Don't complain that you don't have time. If you want to write, you'll make time.

When I began seriously trying to get my work accepted, I was a Deputy Head in a large, demanding comprehensive school; I had a young family at home. It would have been all too easy to have said to myself, I'll write when I get more time. Instead, at the beginning of each week, I would look in my diary and identify an evening (or maybe two) when I was free of meetings or school-related work and write for at least three hours. If I didn't, the only person I was cheating was me. So I persevered. When I talk to writers' groups now, as I occasionally do, I have little patience with the "I haven't got time" argument. If you really want to write, you'll write.

You may find it helpful to join a writers' group, where you can share your work with other like minded people. Many of these groups appear to be made up of aspiring novelists, rather than dramatists, but you may still gain support and encouragement by meeting them regularly.

Above all, write. And when you have finished a script, send it off. Then start another …

That calling card

You may already have a number of scripts to choose from. If not, set yourself a goal: to write a thirty minute TV script, a 60 minute screen play, a 45 minute Radio play, a stage play, something that highlights your strengths and individuality as a writer. Don't try and be the next Alan Bleasdale, Jimmy McGovern, or Paul Abbott, try and be the first you. Writers often talk about "finding their voice" and it is true, it does happen and you'll know when it does. You'll find yourself writing from the heart, about something you know and care about and it will be a wonderful moment.

I have a degree in English from Cambridge University (not a necessary qualification, I hasten to add: writers come from many different backgrounds). I was 36 when my first Radio Play was accepted. By that time I had shed the voices of TS Eliot, James Joyce, Shakespeare and all the great writers I'd studied and found my own voice. Here is the opening of my first broadcast play:

DEREK (SPEAKING OVER MUSIC, WHICH GRADUALLY FADES) I can remember that night. It's as clear as a pint of Tetley's pale mild. I'd been out walking the dog over Woodhouse Moor. I had a lot of time on my hands in those days—on account of not having worked for six months. I must have had the fittest dog in Leeds, the amount of exercise it got. It were a hot, steamy night in late August. I got in about six 'o clock. Oh—my name's Derek—Derek Hargreaves.

It was written in 1985, in the middle of the Thatcher years of austerity. Although I went on to write plays about politics, the environment and racism, my first play was a gentle comedy about cricket, beer, and sex, in a changing world which bemused the central character. It was set in Leeds, my home town and it was a world I knew, inhabited by people I knew.

The calling card

You may already have a body of work from which to choose. If not, get started. And as you want to be a television writer, try writing a pilot for a 30-minute sitcom, or a 60-minute drama series. You could even invent your own Soap and write the opening episode.

3 The bricks and mortar—storyline writing

An overview

Programmes like *Emmerdale* and *Coronation Street*, employ teams of Storyline Writers. There will usually be four or five of them and they are often younger than the script team. Unlike script writers, who work from home, storyline writers are based in the studio base and work under the guidance of the Story Producer or Story Editor. Their task is to take the material generated at a script conference and to turn it into individual documents, each containing the stories to be told in a single episode. At *Emmerdale*, which broadcasts six times a week, this means producing twenty four separate documents in four weeks, between conferences. These documents go to script writers, who are commissioned to write one or two. Storyline writing can be a step on the way to writing scripts. It can also open up avenues into production. This chapter shows you what a storyline looks like and tells you how it is produced.

(In a later chapter I will show you how to turn such a document into a script, but for now, we'll concentrate on the document itself.)

What is a storyline document?

Here is a sample storyline document from *Emmerdale*:

Emmerdale

Episode 5619
WRITER: Chris Thompson

RECORDING:	12th–23rd April 2010
TRANSMISSION:	Thurs 27th May 2010

TX SUNRISE:	0448	VTR SUNRISE:	0602
TX SUNSET:	2120	VTR SUNSET:	2011

Darkness is half an hour before sunrise and half an hour after sunset.

EDNA BIRCH		JOHN BARTON	
EVE BIRCH		MOIRA BARTON	
RODNEY BLACKSTOCK		HOLLY BARTON	
ZAK DINGLE	IN	ADAM BARTON	
SAM DINGLE		NICOLA DE SOUZA	IN
CAIN DINGLE		LEYLA HARDING	IN
DEBBIE DINGLE		PEARL LADDERBANKS	OUT
CHAS DINGLE	IN	LIZZIE LAKELY	
MARLON DINGLE	IN	FAYE LAMB	IN
BETTY EAGLETON	IN	RYAN LAMB	
BOB HOPE		AARON LIVESY	IN
VIV HOPE	IN	DAVID METCALFE	
CARL KING		SANDY THOMAS	
JIMMY KING	IN	BRENDA WALKER	IN
PADDY KIRK	IN	GENNIE WALKER	IN
VAL LAMBERT		ADELE ALLFREY	
ERIC POLLARD		RHONA GOSKIRK	IN
NIKHIL SHARMA	IN	SHADRACH DINGLE	IN
JAI SHARMA	IN	**JUVENILES**	
ANDY SUGDEN		HANNAH BARTON	
DIANE SUGDEN		BELLE DINGLE	
KATIE SUGDEN	IN	SAMSON DINGLE	
CHARITY TATE		ANGELICA KING	
ASHLEY THOMAS		ARTHUR THOMAS	
LAUREL THOMAS		CATHY HOPE	

ALAN TURNER		HEATH HOPE	
TERRY WOODS	IN	SARAH SUGDEN	
NATASHA WYLDE	IN	VICTORIA SUGDEN	
MAISIE WYLDE		GABRIELLE THOMAS	
NATHAN WYLDE		NOAH TATE	
CHARLIE		TJ WOODS	
DECLAN	IN	WILL WYLDE	
WAYNE	IN		
TOTAL CHARACTERS	22	**TOTAL JUVENILES**	0

- **Aaron faces genuine homophobia.**
- Viv bans Bob from seeing the kids.
- Jai and Nikhil see Declan is keen on Natasha.

Hook: Homophobes lash out at Aaron.

A) Aaron

P/U: Adam and Aaron plan to hit a gay bar tonight.

AARON's in a surly mood as he heads out of Smithy to go on community service. Ignoring an acerbic remark from **BETTY,** supportive **PADDY** guesses it's quite humiliating working in a public park. Aaron retorts he couldn't give a stuff where he has to do it. Trying to be nice, **RHONA** asks if he's made any mates but Aaron shoots them a stony, telling look and walks off. Paddy's uneasy to see Aaron's finding it tough.

Outside the factory on a break, **GENNIE** is too despondent to care as **CHAS** witters on to her about how fed up Carl seems with the hassle surrounding Aaron. Spotting **SHADRACH** and **ZAK** passing, Chas confronts Shadrach about being out of order last night. Glancing warily at Zak, Shadrach edgily denies but Gennie agrees she noticed it too. Chas dryly reckons Shadrach's not one for subtleties and questions what his problem is. Claiming to be busy, Shadrach slopes off.

Aaron wanders over to the group of lads and immediately senses he was being talked about. As the community service officer starts divvying them into groups, Aaron sees the lads' hostile glares and begins to start feeling paranoid.

Having dinner in the pub, Gennie is fretting to an unsympathetic Chas about Viv when Shadrach comes in with Zak. Blunt, Chas reckons he doesn't appear to be 'busy' now and awaits answers. Shadrach clumsily admits he can't understand why Aaron is suddenly gay when he had a girlfriend not long ago. Zak looks uneasy and Gennie defensively insists Aaron can't help who he is. Shadrach is sure it isn't right, none of the Dingle men have been gay. Stunned, Chas can't believe after everything Aaron's gone through, his own granddad could be so narrow-minded.

Taking a break, the lads are eating butties in the park when they see two girls sat on a bench eating their lunch. Showing off to the others, **WAYNE** makes a sexist comment about one of them. Trying to fit in, Aaron coolly claims she was eyeing him up. Weighing Aaron up, Wayne challenges him to go and chat her up then. As the lads voice their agreement, Aaron masks his nerves as he coolly heads across to where they are sitting.

Aaron's floundering as the girl cringes at his hopeless attempt to chat her up. Listening, the lads jeeringly encourage Aaron who tries to conceal his awkwardness with an overly macho front. When the girl loses her patience and gives him short shrift, Aaron is visibly relieved. Heading back to the lads, Aaron sees them smirking. Wayne cockily guesses Aaron failed because he's queer, he read all about him in the paper. Aaron is utterly thrown.

Terrified at being exposed, Aaron firmly denies he is gay. Disbelieving, Wayne makes a snide comment and Aaron darkly reckons if Wayne read the article then he'll know he was in court for beating up sick, gay men. Wayne is enjoying his power trip but Aaron coldly cuts him dead, claiming he only said he was a bender to avoid prison. As the lads seemingly buy it, Aaron is rocked by the depths he will plummet to avoid being 'found out'.

Aaron's desperate for the day to end when he hears the lads whistling at another woman. Hearing the approaching totter of heels, Aaron is thrown to see Chas stroll up and brightly ask how it is going. Cringing, Aaron grits his teeth and tells her he is fine and she should go. Aware she's embarrassed him, Chas awkwardly insists she just wanted to check he was okay. As Chas slopes off, Wayne sneeringly laughs at the mummy's boy.

Filled with self-loathing, Aaron heads into the shed to return his spade. Aaron is about to head out when he hears the door slam shut and a roar of laughter from outside. Rushing to the door, Aaron tries to open it but it's locked. Hearing Wayne's homophobic ridiculing outside, Aaron angrily brays at the door and warns they better let him out. As the laughter increases, Aaron kicks the door repeatedly in frustration. Aware he's being bullied for the first time in his life, Aaron is rocked by the depth of his own vulnerability.

B) Viv, Bob & Gennie

P/U: Viv wants a divorce and custody of the children.

At Tall Trees, Bob is desperate and furious. Yesterday he was hopeful of reconciliation, but now Viv wants a divorce and the kids. **MARLON** knows Viv can't deny Bob access to the twins and wonders if he's still going to fight for his marriage. Bob wanted to, but Viv is too volatile. He knows he started this, but it should all have stayed buried. It was her jealous, vindictive behaviour that has escalated this out of all proportion. Despite what Viv says, Bob has no intention of keeping away from the kids.

TERRY comes into the shop to find a determined **VIV** fending off Betty who is fishing for gossip. Viv claims now she's made the decision to file for divorce, it feels like a weight has been lifted off her shoulders. Insisting Viv doesn't need to put on a façade for him, Terry knows Bob was, and is, the love of Viv's life and refuses to believe she this is truly what she wants. Cold, Viv reckons once the love of your life has cheated on you with someone half your age, there's no going back and Bob has to pay the price.

Meeting for a drink at dinnertime, Gennie feels sick as she recounts the playground incident yesterday to **KATIE** and **LEYLA**. Gennie frets that it would be best all round if she went off and had a fresh start alone. Insisting she mustn't make a snap decision, Katie thinks she needs time to sort her head out first. Reckoning running away wouldn't help her forget Jamie anyway, Leyla thinks instead of mourning the end of her relationship she should have fun with them and suggests a girly night in. **BRENDA** sees the girls rallying round Gennie and curtly requests a word.

Terry finds Bob distressed outside the village hall playgroup. He's come to see the twins, but Viv has had him taken off the carers list. There to pick up Angelica, **JIMMY** can't help feeling for Bob as he hopelessly explains how he could hear Cathy and Heath's voices as they played, but he couldn't see them. Sympathetic, Terry offers to have a word with Mrs Cowling, but Bob knows it's Viv he has to tackle.

Outside the pub, Brenda bluntly informs Gennie that Viv is filing for a divorce. Rocked, Gennie thinks Viv is going too far, certain what happened between her and Bob isn't worth splitting up a family for. Unable to mask her disdain, Brenda wishes Gennie had thought about that before jumping into bed with Bob and hopes she's proud of herself. Aware Brenda used to harbour feelings for Bob too, Gennie knows how much she's let her down. Not ready to forgive, Brenda walks away. Gennie feels forlorn.

Jimmy is cajoling Bob to come for a drink when they clock Viv loading the kids into the car. Rushing over, Bob tries to see the twins but Viv insists they are late for the solicitors. Bob's furious and warns she's the one with the prison record so is more in danger of losing the kids than him. Jimmy steps in to calm things but Viv fumes Bob will leave the twins eventually, like he left all his kids. She wants to save them the pain, they're young enough to forget him. Hurting, Bob urges her to go for a divorce, but he'll stay there and fight.

C) Home Farm

P/U: Natasha warned Declan to watch out for Cain.

At Home Farm, **DECLAN** arrives in and cracks a joke about seeing **NICOLA** concealing a wedding brochure, thinking it's enough she gets to hold her wedding reception there.

Nicola is glad to see Declan's not going to tell her off for skiving and questions his good mood. His attentions on **NATASHA**, Declan excuses he's just got a good feeling about things. His mood changes however when he opens a letter from the council, explaining someone's voiced an objection to his application for planning permission.

In the pub, Natasha's amused by Declan's passion for this project as he irritably insists he isn't going to let it slip through his fingers, (he's the antithesis of Mark). Seeing **JAI** and **NIKHIL** arrive in with **FAYE**, Declan immediately collars Jai to chat about his planning problems and Nikhil sidles up to casually chat to Maisie about a new film that's on at the cinema tomorrow. Suddenly left alone with Faye, Natasha is awkward and invents an excuse to leave. Declan clocks the tension between them.

Declan clocks a flirtatious Faye and Jai leaving the factory and casually hopes he didn't put her in an awkward position with Natasha earlier. Smiling edgily, Faye admits though they can deal with living in the same village, she and Natasha's history is still too raw to warrant small talk. Declan hopes things might get easier between them, as he and Jai are good mates and would be nice to feel they could all go out sometime. (XR Jai & Faye) Exchanging a charged look with Faye, Jai is already two steps in front of Declan. Playing it cool, Faye casually agrees it might be possible, one day.

D) Faye and Jai

P/U: Faye and Jai shared a meal together at Holdgate.

At the factory, Jai is going over paperwork with Faye when she sees an invite to a business function tonight. Jai reckons it's just a chance for a booze up and wonders if she fancies going too. Laughing, Faye reckons it's the ultimate cliché taking his PA along. Sensing a frisson of chemistry between them, Jai thinks clichés can sometimes be fun. Coming in, Nikhil senses he's interrupted something as Jai and Faye attempt to resume normality.

Leaving for dinner, Faye's advising a glum Gennie to try and steer clear of Viv for now when Jai calls her back—she's forgotten something. As Gennie heads off, Faye returns and Jai gives her a flirtatious smile, questioning if she's going to take him up on his offer of a date or not. Amused, Faye teases that it's a *'date'* now and insists she couldn't ever be so unprofessional. With a touch of sexual tension, Jai jokingly pulls rank, claiming he needs her there in case he needs notes taking. Loving the chase, Faye agrees in that case, she can't refuse. Jai's made up.

What do you notice?

As a quick task, write down your reactions to the document. Does it surprise you in any way? What features stand out? Is there anything you don't understand?

De-coding the document

You'll notice that the episode was to be recorded between the 12th and 23rd April 2010 and was broadcast on May 27th. What it doesn't say, is that the episode was commissioned (i.e., given to me to write) on January 29th. The first draft was due on February 16th, the second on March 9th and the final edit was on March 19th, when the Director had his input, the third draft was written in a couple of days and the script was finally "put to bed." (i.e., given to the actors and key members of the crew).

TX is an abbreviation for Transmission.

VTR is abbreviation for Video Tape recording i.e., the dates on which the episode will be recorded.

The times of sunrise and sunset are crucial to the recording schedule and are guidelines for the scriptwriter when structuring the episode. (See later chapter).

P/U is short for Pick-Up, in other words the point at which the story was left in a previous episode.

After the cast list, the main story headings are listed, with the A story in bold.

The process

Before the storyline writers begin work on the documents, they will meet and establish a number of priorities, under the direction of the Story Producer.

Which 'A' strand stories are going to feature in the 24 episodes? These will be the headline grabbing, big stories that form the dramatic spine of the block. Some will be the payoff to long running stories, some will present twists and turns in established stories, others may bring new stories to the forefront of the programme.

Remember, some stories will run for several months, years even, and it is the story liners' task to keep those stories fresh and surprising, to extract the maximum drama from them and to keep the audience involved and interested, wondering what is going to happen next. Pacing is vital. Stories mustn't flag; neither must they go on for too long. (The A story in this episode centres around Aaron, a young man struggling with his sexuality. "Coming out" stories aren't new but this one was told with an originality and emotional power that received accolades from Stonewall, the Gay Rights Pressure Group and won awards for the actor playing Aaron, Danny Miller.)

Each episode has to have a strong Hook (or Tag or Cliff Hanger). The final beat of an episode should leave the audience eager to know what is going to happen next, so they'll switch on for the next episode. These Hooks will be borne in mind when the month's episodes are being planned and plotted. Occasionally, a Hook will be the close of a story (someone dies, gets arrested or married, for instance) but more often the intention is to lead in to the next episode.

I have in the past heard the plaintive cry from the Story Editor on day three of a conference "we haven't got enough tags". That makes the job of his/her team difficult. Tags don't have to be melodramatic or heightened, but they have to have sufficient emotional and dramatic strength to conclude the episode.

You will notice that other stories are listed as B, C, D and so forth. These are the stories which support and surround the A story. They may be stories which are being seeded for later development, long running stories which are being kept bubbling along, or maybe short arc stories, which run for two or three blocks only.

In planning the block of stories, the storyline team has to bear in mind a number of other issues: some actors may be unavailable, because of leave, or illness. Some actors, featuring in a big story, may be in danger of being over used. There are only so many hours in a day and the story team have to avoid making too many demands on particular actors.

Audiences become attached to characters and like to see them regularly. In the story planning process, it is important to keep some characters on screen, even if they are not involved in big stories. At the same time, it can be demoralising for actors if they appear only to order a drink in the pub or buy a loaf of bread in the shop. At conference, writers may be told if certain characters are slipping under the radar and being underused. Finding them a story becomes a priority. If it happens a few times, it may be an indicator that certain characters have run their course and there are no more stories left to play. It doesn't happen often, but occasionally that reality has to be faced.

Some stories will cross in scripts. This will be made clear when we look at how the storyline is changed into a script. It is why Soaps have communal sets and locations, where groups of characters can interact and cross and three or four separate strands.

Finally, when the storylined episode reaches the screen several months later, it will almost certainly have changed, sometimes quite significantly. There could be several reasons for this: once the story begins to be told through scripts, fault lines may appear and the decision will be taken to tell the story a different way; individual writers may bring different ideas to specific strands; a story may simply not work, or a new, more exciting idea may emerge. Later on in the book, I will track a scene through three drafts, to show how this process works.

THE STORYLINE IS ONE STAGE IN AN EVOLVING PROCESS WHICH BRINGS AN EPISODE TO SCREEN. THE INTENTION IS ALWAYS TO TELL STORIES IN THE MOST DRAMATIC AND ENGAGING WAY POSSIBLE.

Remember, working on a storyline team is a tried and trusted way into writing Soap. The teams change quite regularly and the programmes from time to time run workshops, giving aspiring story liners experience of the process. These can lead to jobs, so don't discount this as a career path.

A brief task

Watch an episode of your favourite Soap and record it. Using it as a starting point, write a storyline for the following episode, using the same groups of characters. You'll note that each story strand has a number of "beats" i.e., moments which progress the story and/or our understanding of characters.

There is a constant tension in Soaps, between being character led, plot led or issue led. The ideal Soap would combine all three. If an episode is too plot led, there will be little time for character development or texture; if character dominates at the expense of plot, then viewers may feel that "nothing happens". You also need to be aware that although Soaps deal with issues, from coming out, to anorexia, to drug addiction, they should be firmly rooted in character, to avoid being seen as public information broadcasts or documentaries.

The job

Let's say you land a storyline job on one of the major Soaps. What will your job entail?

You will be based in a story office in the Production Centre. You will have your own desk and computer and will share the office with your fellow storyline writers. You will attend the two or three day story conferences and be expected to take notes on what is said. You may from time to time have to act as "official recorder" and note the key contributions and decisions directly on to a lap top.

After the conference is finished, you will meet with your fellow story liners and assess the material which has emerged. At *Emmerdale*, a white board is used to track the shape of the four week block, looking at where major stories can be played. Some of this will be determined by the pace of the story up to that point. It could be appropriate to "look away" from some but to dive straight into others, playing them high in the mix. Getting the balance right across the block of episodes, is vital.

You will in all probability be given responsibility for certain story strands across the block. This means that those stories will have continuity and gives you the opportunity to shape and develop the story. It is also a chance to express yourself as a writer. You have to write to a fixed brief, but the way you tell the story will say something about your skills and strengths. At a later stage, the various stories will be married together to form individual episodes. (It is a common misconception that scriptwriters work in the same way. As I said earlier, we don't, we write whole episodes, telling all the stories within them).

The storyline documents will go through edits, just like scripts. The Series Producer will want to read them and be satisfied that they are taking shape in the way he or she envisaged. They will be commissioned to various writers to write and sent out a few days before the next script conference.

If you join a story team, be prepared to work long hours, especially as the deadline for delivering the story document approaches. It can be exhausting work, but you have a vital role to play in the making of the programme.

A fantastic opportunity

If you join the story team, you have the chance to learn first-hand how the programme is made, from the story process to the screen. You will be in the production centre and get to meet directors, actors and the other vital members of the team. You will learn how to shape a story over time, how stories are pitched, which stories work and which don't, the strengths and weaknesses of various characters, in short, you will get to know the programme inside out. This puts you in a strong position if you have ambitions to write scripts. A significant number of my colleagues over the years have got their opportunity to write for the show via this route. After serving their time in the story office, they have asked for the opportunity to write a trial script and been invited to join the script writing team. From the Producer's point of view, this makes a lot of sense: they are giving the job to someone who is familiar with the programme and how it is made.

So if you do get the chance to be a story liner, make the most of it: listen to the ebb and flow of ideas at conference, join in if you feel able to; ask if you can read scripts, to see how different writers approach the job; make yourself useful, be reliable and dependable. There is always the possibility that your trial script won't make it, but you will have learned a lot that will stand you in good stead. Storyline writers can also progress to be script editors, story editors and series producers.

One more task

Choose a group of characters from your favourite Soap. Write a free standing story strand, for a week, a month, however long it takes to tell the story you think of. Be aware of the need to keep the story moving and be conscious of the need to have peaks, which can provide end of episode hooks.

Do I have to talk as well?

How to survive the script conference

An overview

Soaps devour stories and need a constant supply to keep the programme fresh and the viewers interested. To meet this need, some continuing dramas hold regular script conferences. Stories have to come from somewhere and sitting a group of writers round a conference table for two to three days is as good a way as any. You may find this an opportunity to shine, as you are brim-full of ideas and confident in your ability to convey them. Or you may view the prospect with dread, talking in front of an audience of twenty or thirty critical listeners being your idea of hell.

Not all continuing dramas hold such conference, but if you work on one that does, you need to be ready.

How do they work?

When I wrote for BBC Radio 4 FM's *The Archers*, we met for one day each month, in Birmingham. Twice a year we would have long term planning conferences, which involved two days and an overnight stay. Other programmes I have worked on, like *Families*, *Revelations* and *Children's Ward* usually involved one day conferences.

When I first worked on *Emmerdale*, in 1998, the programme was on three times per week. We used to meet once every three weeks, for one and a half days, and twice a year we would have longer conferences for long term planning.

Nowadays, with the programme going out six times a week, we meet once every month for two and a half days, which means two overnight stays. Long term conferences now happen four times a year, for three days.

You can either look upon this as a negative, begrudging being dragged away from the safety of your office and lap top for two or three days, or you can embrace the positive. Writing is essentially a solitary occupation. Writing on a Soap means you can get to meet like-minded people, share your passions and ideas, stay up half the night in the hotel bar, talking about the programme (if you have the stamina) and make a real contribution to the shape and direction of the show.

I have always been in the latter camp. Eighteen years teaching in comprehensive schools means I am not backwards at coming forwards and I have enjoyed the cut—and—thrust and hurly burly of conference. I have also made some lifelong friendships, although my late night hotel bar sessions are a thing of the past.

The structure

You will find yourself sitting round a table with anything upwards of ten or twelve people. These days on *Emmerdale* it is often upwards of thirty.

The conference is chaired by the Series Producer, who will have the final say on which stories are told and how they are told. The Story Producer and her/his team of storyline writers will be there, as will the Script Producer and (for some of the time) the script editors. The script writers make up the bulk of the attendees, and there may also be the programme researcher.

The first session will usually be the commissioning conference. A few days prior to the conference, 24 episodes will have been allocated to writers in storyline form. The writers will have produced a scene-by-scene breakdown and the commissioning conference gives them, the opportunity to raise any questions they might have or to argue for any changes they might like to make. (There is more about this in a later chapter).

The bulk of the conference is about planning stories.

SHORT TERM

Writers receive an agenda a few days before conference. It will indicate the stories that need attention at short term; by that I mean to plan the next stages in an agreed long-term story over the next four weeks. (Remember what is discussed will not be on screen for four months or so). Stories are not set in stone at long-term, they evolve in the telling and the short-term conference is where the detailed story beats are plotted. It may well include discussion of where in the block of four weeks the story will play in relation to other stories and how many tags it will provide across that block.

LONG-TERM

This is essentially a blank canvas, and producers are looking for big, bold stories which will have the legs to run for months or even years. Written pitches are invited ahead of conference and spoken pitches can be delivered around the table. If you pitch a story in advance, you will be expected to argue for it. If you care about the story, you'll want to argue for it.

Even at short-term conference, new stories can be pitched. As I said before, the agenda may indicate which characters are in need of a story, those who have maybe played a big story in the recent past but have slipped into the background.

To paraphrase the former British Prime Minister, one Tony Blair, it's story, story, story ….

Plan and prepare

When you arrive on a Soap, unless you have watched it from day one, you are at a disadvantage, when it comes to pitching stories. When programmes have run as long as *Coronation Street*, *Emmerdale* and *Eastenders*, they will have told an awful lot of stories. You may put hours of effort into planning and preparing a story, send in the document, be invited to speak to it, only for some old hand to pipe up, "we've done that …"

You can minimise the chances of this happening, by a phone call to the story office, the archivist, or a fellow writer, and asking if a similar story has been told recently or in the dim and distant past.

When it comes to deciding which stories to pitch, you will have your own reasons. Some writers grow attached to particular characters and tend to suggest stories for them. You may feel strongly about certain characters and be bursting to tell stories about them.

The written pitch

Written pitches can come in all shapes and sizes. Some writers spend hours plotting and structuring their story, almost scene-by-scene. The pitch can run to several pages. I would advise against it. A story pitched at long-term if accepted, will almost certainly change and evolve in the telling. The best advice I was given was to limit a story pitch to no more than one side of A4, giving bullet points only and giving the story a title. The title gives a flavour of what is to come; simply putting a family name at the top of the page does not.

A successful pitch can be one sentence. "*A*" *falls in love with his best friend's girlfriend*. If those two characters are well-established and well-loved, then you have a story, which can run for a long time, changing lives. (I pitched exactly that story at *Emmerdale* called, with homage to Elvis Presley, *The Girl of My Best Friend*).

Less is more.

The verbal pitch

If you can do it, then pitching a story without a written document, without notes, can be the most effective way of all. It takes planning, it takes confidence, but it can win hearts and influence people.

The rough and tumble

Don't expect the Queensbury rules around the table. Some writers choose to sit in virtual silence throughout a conference, but if you want to get involved in the decision making process—and you should—then you have to be prepared to open your mouth and take your chances. You run the risk of having your carefully crafted story or your telling contribution to the debate swatted away or ignored, but if you care, you'll come back for more.

You have twenty or more people round the table, many of whom want to speak at the same time. A good producer will make sure that everyone gets their chance to speak, but some writers feel fazed by the situation. Writers rightly feel strongly about characters and about stories and will fight passionately to get their point of view across. I've always regarded it as part of the job. After all, if no one spoke, there wouldn't be any story, save those handed down from on high. Besides, what's the point of being on the team if you never kick the ball?

Pecking orders—real and imagined

Stories about conference tables are legion: people storming out in a rage, or in tears; apples being thrown across the room and people turning up first thing in the morning the worse for wear and so on ...

You may also hear words of advice: never speak at your first conference; don't sit in such and such a chair, as it belongs to the Big Beast ...

Well, I did speak at my first TV script conference (which was in 1991) and it didn't do me any harm. I haven't stopped talking since. I was (once) accused of Mickey Mouse story telling (it didn't happen again) and I have seen people walk out of a conference (I did it myself once). And I have witnessed some fairly brutal put-downs.

But this isn't a safe office job; it's a competitive business, full of creative people with strong feelings and opinions. That's what makes it so exhilarating. My advice would be to find your own way of negotiating conference: you may want to spend the first one watching and learning. But if you have something you want to say, say it. Don't be afraid to come up with stories: sooner or later, you'll hear approving sounds from round the table and you'll feel like you've arrived. But do get involved, don't be a spectator. You'll find life much more fulfilling.

Before moving on to look at the types of stories you could pitch, bear in mind a few cautionary notes:

Differentiate between a situation and a story

X takes over the shop from Y, is a SITUATION. X forms an alliance with Z behind Y's back, and runs a dirty tricks campaign to undermine the business, before buying it for a knock-down price, is a STORY.

I once sat round a conference table where a fellow writer said, and I paraphrase, "Lady B is sitting in her bathtub, surrounded by candles, sipping champagne". We waited to hear what came next, but nothing did. One (albeit attractive) image, total screen time about 10 seconds!

Be true to character. The audience (and the actor playing that character) will know the character better than you. If you are going to turn the lovable loser into an axe murderer, then you'd better have your reasons.

Don't be too reliant on bringing in new characters. Soaps need new characters, but they need to provide story for their long-standing, much-loved, established characters.

5 Once upon a time

An overview

So what stories are you going to pitch? What is going to make the producer sit up and take notice and earn the respect of the old hands who've heard (and written) it all before?

Many writers will tell you they love writing dialogue and they can come up with any number of sparky and original characters, but what they can't do is write plot. The mechanics of storytelling defeat them. Someone famously once said that there are basically only seven plots and every work of fiction is essentially a variation on one of those themes.

A couple come to mind immediately: the star-crossed lovers, with Romeo and Juliet as the presiding spirits and the idea of revenge, wanting to right a perceived wrong.

As I said in the previous chapter, Soaps greedily devour plots and stories. Think about how many times they are on our screens each week, and for how many years. Calculating the number of stories told would be an impossible task.

Several times a year, as a writer, I am asked (as we all are) to come up with long-term stories. And it is hard. But, if you want to do this job, put yourself in my place. You sit there, with the cast list in front of you and a blank piece of paper or a flickering cursor on an empty screen.

Where do you begin?

I look for characters who have maybe been under the radar for a while, who are capable of carrying big stories but have perhaps been a bit quiet on screen for a while.

I mull over the things they have been doing on screen recently, I recall their history, I think of the characters they interact with.

I ask myself a number of questions. Is there a recurring pattern of behaviour that I could pick up on? Conversely, is it time for this character, or group of characters to behave out of character? Is there an opportunity to play them with characters they wouldn't normally interact with? Is it time for someone new or someone from their past to enter or re-enter their life? Is it time for their out story? Is there something in the ether, in the zeitgeist that I can see playing out in the programme?

Basic principles

Having identified a character or character group for whom I want to pitch a story, I have to shape a story within the parameters of a Soap. That means bearing in mind a number of things that are different about Soap storytelling.

In a film a story is told in two hours or so, in a TV Drama, it may be over two to six hour long episodes. In a Soap, a story may run for **YEARS.** This has a huge impact on the way you plot your story.

Before moving on, let me give an example. When the Wylde family came to Home Farm in *Emmerdale* early in 2009, there were two parents in their fifties, Mark and Natasha, two grown up children, Nathan and Maise and 11-year old Will Before they arrived on screen, the writing team had devised an intricate back story. Namely that Mark Wylde had left behind a previous identity, Daniel Lamb, twenty years ago. He had also left behind a wife and a son he never knew about. After a few months establishing themselves in the village, Mark's first wife, Faye discovered he was still alive and came to find him, with their son, Ryan. The ramifications of that return included murder, blackmail, and near-incest and provided story that spread beyond the confines of Home Farm for two years.

And the fact is, that was PLANNED, it didn't just happen. Not every single beat was plotted from day one; those details were finessed in monthly meetings but what was produced was a **STORY ARC.**

As the name suggests, the arc is the overall shape of the story, the framework, if you like, on which the story can be placed and developed. You need to be clear when planning a story, that it has an arc, that it goes somewhere. A common mistake, and not just among new writers, is to mistake a **SITUATION** for a story. (See my example above. A situation may be created by putting a group of characters together, in a new relationship, house or job, but if nothing else happens, it isn't a story).

Not every story you pitch will have such a long arc. You may pitch a story that will play over two or three blocks, but you should develop an instinct for the length and pace of a story. Sometimes, you may pitch such a short term story and your fellow writers will run with it, get excited about it and turn a short term story into something much more substantial. Once you throw a story into the ring, you have to be prepared to let it go. It becomes part of the collective process. If you feel strongly, you will fight hard to preserve the elements you feel are vital but you have to be prepared to let go a little.

You need to bear in mind a few other basic ideas.

Your story should have **IMPACT**; it should change people's lives. If, at the end of the story, life goes on much as before, then what was the point of telling the story?

The story should progress in a **NON-LINEAR** way. There should be surprises along the way, twists and turns, to keep the audience engaged and interested.

The story may start with two or three people but it will work best if its consequences spread beyond the main protagonists, and impact on the lives of other people. *Emmerdale*, *Weatherfield* and *Walford* are close communities and people gossip, get involved, become innocent bystanders …

Tried and trusted

I said at the top of this chapter that there are certain plots which recur throughout literature. And it isn't simply because there isn't that many to choose from, it's also because they work. They are the types of story have a timeless, and universal appeal. And the same applies to the stories we tell in Soap. Certain plots come up time and time again and the challenge of the Soap writer is to find new ways of telling them. And there's no reason why popular drama shouldn't look to classical literature for inspiration: is there a better love story than Romeo and Juliet, a better exploration of jealousy than Othello, a better illustration of the destructive power of ambition than Macbeth?

On a less exalted level, I once based an hour long episode of *Emmerdale* on the story of Cinderella, while remaining true to the characters and style of the show. It was nominated for a BAFTA, so keep your eyes open for inspiration.

Affairs

Affairs are one of the staples of Soap and allow the viewer the vicarious thrill of watching someone risk everything as they embark on an ill-advised liaison, throwing caution to the winds and allowing lust to govern their actions.

However, the fact is that affairs on TV can be dull, if not handled properly. We can't, quite rightly, go into the bedroom as explicitly, as we could in a film, so we have to portray the danger and excitement in other ways.

Before coming up with an affair story, you should ask yourself the following questions:

Do we feel sympathy for any of the protagonists? If so, whom? Logic would suggest we feel for the person who is being betrayed, but that may be the obvious route. What will be the consequences of the affair? A marriage destroyed; lives ruined, or worse? Murder has been committed as a result of infidelity. Is the affair instigated by a "love rat", a serial philanderer perhaps and if so, does he or she get their comeuppance?

What is at stake?

This can provide a classic example of mistaking a situation for a story. Putting X with Y might seem sexy and dangerous but what are the consequences?

Who shot ...?

You may remember the legendary eighties American Soap *Dallas*, where *Who Shot JR?* became an iconic story. Anticipated and watched by millions, the audience was captivated and enthralled as the shooting took place and kept switching on subsequently to learn the identity of the killer.

It is a story which has been repeated successfully in British Soap, most notably in *Eastenders*, with Phil Mitchell as the victim, while *Emmerdale* killed Tom King, not by shooting but by being hit over the head and then falling through a window.

This isn't the sort of story that can happen too often. The world of Soap is not the Wild West. But it can work brilliantly.

If you were to pitch such a story you'd have to bear in mind a number of issues.

The victim has to be someone of real status and clout in the programme. His or her death or attempted murder should have major implications. You need to decide if they are indeed going to die, or survive. To get maximum impact from the story, you have to have a number of plausible suspects, each with a motive for wishing the victim harm. These motives will need to be established in the weeks and months prior to the incident. You will want to place a few red herrings before the viewer, teasing them before revealing the true identity of the assailant. And when that identity is revealed, you have to decide if you wish to keep that character in the programme. And if you do, how can you realistically show them avoiding justice?

We all love a whodunit and this type of story allows you as a writer to bring out your inner Agatha Christie.

Disasters

From time to time Soaps may choose to play big, set-piece disasters. They are intended to be visually spectacular, but underneath the mayhem and destruction, stories have to be told, lives affected and, in some cases, ended. Again, some basic questions need to be asked before embarking on such a story. Is the disaster someone's fault, the result of human error or incompetence? When a new house collapsed in *Emmerdale* some years ago, it was the result of cost cutting by the Kings; the bolt of lightning which caused the pub to collapse on Tricia, was an *Act-of-God*. You need to decide which it is to be. In story telling terms the disaster itself will often spread over several episodes, being told almost in real time. On one level, this is a way of gaining maximum value for money, out of what will be an expensive stunt. But it also allows several different story strands to cross.

By definition, disasters affect the lives of many people. So who are those people going to be? If someone is going to die, who will it be? As I said earlier, it has to be someone whose death has consequences. How will those left behind cope with the disaster? Will it be the start of another story for one or more of the protagonists?

I've got a bit of a head ache ...

A colleague of mine, a very experienced writer, is fond of reminding the rest of us about how switched on our audience is. They have come to recognise certain signs. So, if a woman meets a man for the first time and later complains to her friend that she can't stand him, we take that as code, meaning they are bound to have an affair. Similarly, if a character complains of a headache, we can assume she will have a brain tumour.

It's a frivolous way into what is a serious area for Soap storytelling. It is the job of Soap to reflect life and illness is a part of life. So Soaps have tackled cases of life threatening illness, like heart disease, strokes and cancer. It is an area which needs to be approached with great care and sensitivity. Most of the audience will have first or second hand experience of serious illness, affecting them or members of their family. So, the first priority is to make sure the medical research is accurate. Details of symptoms, treatment, likely chances of recovery, need to be spot on, or it could call real distress.

When tackling such subjects, Soaps feel a certain responsibility to send out a positive and hopeful message to people who may be struggling with illness. So it is often the case that cancer sufferers, for instance, recover, as many do, of course, in real life. Now and again, though, the character may not recover and that puts an extra burden of responsibility on the programme. If pitching a story like this, you need, of course, to decide who is going to fall ill. And you need to decide what the story is. If Soaps simply traced the course of the illness and treatment, they would be doing the job of a documentary. As writers, we have to be alive to the impact that illness will have on other people, on the people who love and care for that character, and show how it will change lives, for better or worse.

You will often hear at the end of an episode dealing with an illness, an invitation to contact a help line for people who may be experiencing similar problems. It is a sign of the reach that Soaps have and the good that they can do. During my time on *Emmerdale* we have tackled both bowel and testicular cancer, and both times have been thanked by medical professionals for our sensitive handling of the topics. In the case of testicular cancer, we were told that we had encouraged more men to go and be checked by their GP. So Soap isn't all froth, not by any means.

Coming out

Not too many years ago, homosexuality would have been a taboo subject for pre-watershed television. Nowadays, most Soaps will have established gay characters in their casts and will have told several stories featuring gay characters, during the course of their history. *Eastenders* with Colin Russell, *Emmerdale* with Zoe Tate and *Coronation Street*'s Sean Tully have all played significant parts in their respective programmes.

Sean arrived in *Weatherfield* as an out and proud gay man, but Soaps have tended to look at coming out, the pressures and difficulties faced by (often) young people coming to terms with their sexuality. The experiences of Aaron Livesey in *Emmerdale*, who raged, sometimes violently, against who he was, were powerfully told and played and earned the actor many deserved plaudits.

However, there is a real opportunity beyond a coming out story, to integrate gay characters further into the fabric of

Soaps. The challenge, which I don't think has been fully met, is to tell stories involving gay characters, which have nothing whatsoever to do with their sexuality. In other words, to allow them the full range of story opportunities we afford to heterosexual characters.

Killers, serial or otherwise

Richard Hillman, the serial killer of *Weatherfield*, was a ground-breaking and deservedly iconic Soap character. Unlike the *"Who Shot …?"* model, the audience knew what Hillman was and what he had done. So the story had a different dynamic, as the audience wondered who would be his next victim and if and when he would get his comeuppance. The story climaxed with Gail, one of the programme's most loved characters, and her children, being placed in real jeopardy, as he drove them all into the canal.

Murder is part of drama and murderous passions will be aroused in Soaps. If you choose to pitch a story involving a murder, you have the option, as with Richard Hillman, to let the audience in on it at an early stage. It is, if you like, the Columbo model, as made famous by the portrayal of the TV cop *Columbo* by the actor Peter Falk. So what keeps the audience hooked is wondering if he or she will strike again and if they will get caught.

As a way of telling a story, this is potentially trickier than the whodunit. It is harder to keep the suspense at a pitch, as the audience is in on the secret, but it can work brilliantly, as the Hillman story proves. The key is to make your killer plausible, an accepted member if the community and to make sure that you place a popular and well-liked character in his sights. Then we'll be rooting for them, hoping they'll survive.

Issues

Over the years, Soaps have dealt with many social issues: rape, assisted suicide, alcoholism, drug abuse and domestic violence, to name but a few. And there is a place for this type of hard-hitting social realism in the tapestry of stories that make up a Soap. But, as with stories featuring illness, it is important to remember that the research serves the story and that the story should be led by the **CHARACTER** and not the issue.

Such stories are, by their very nature, controversial and raise moral issues, which the programme has to address. For instance, in real life, many rapists escape scot free, their crimes never even coming to trial, many not even reported. How should a Soap deal with that dilemma? Assisted suicide divides opinion: some people believe it is unacceptable in any circumstances, others that it is a basic human right to choose when to die. Is it possible to show an established character being guilty of domestic violence and somehow redeem him (or her)? How far can one go in showing the realities of drug and alcohol abuse and their impact on families and loved ones?

I offer no answers at this point. But, if you were interested in pitching a story along these lines, you would have to decide how you would answer these questions. Much could depend on the character you choose to carry the stories. A well-loved character behaving appallingly might be easier to redeem than one who is universally disliked.

These are all questions fundamental to storytelling, and, as in other areas, you should bear in mind the impact and the consequences of these events.

A task

You should by now have all the ammunition you need to put together a story pitch. Following my guidelines of one side of A4, bullet points and a title, write a written story pitch for your Soap of choice. This will prove invaluable should you ever get to meet a Producer who is interested in you.

And remember the following key points:

Make sure your story has legs. It doesn't have to be a two year blockbuster, but it has to be worth telling. It may be a two month romantic comedy, but it needs to have progression, to have elements of surprise and twists and turns. It needs an ARC.

Try to tell a story which crosses different family and character groups. Telling a good story is like casting a pebble into a pond. It ripples outwards, affecting people, possibly the whole community, changing lives. A story should have consequences. If at the end, nothing has changed, then what was the point of telling it?

6 Your chance to shine—the trial script

An overview

By now, you should know what you're letting yourself in for. By whatever route you travelled, you have arrived in the Producer's office. He or she will have read some of your work and be seriously considering offering you a place on the team. But first, unless you are an established writer (and in some cases, even if you are) you will be asked to write a trial script. You will be given a published storyline, like the one in Chapter 3 and sent away to write it. As I said before, it will most likely be one that has already been turned into a script by one of the team. You may be given a sample script to help you with layout and you may be given a deadline but then it's up to you.

Do you have all the ammunition?

You should be familiar with the show. Even if you hadn't watched the programme regularly before, as soon as you contacted the Producer, you should have started watching it, every episode. You should know the characters and have a feel for the rhythms of their speech. You should be up to speed with the stories currently being told on the programme. You should be comfortable with the tone and style of the programme. If you have any further questions or have any uncertainties, now is the time to bring them up. Once you leave that office, you're on your own.

You are ready to start. One final word of advice: as I said earlier, the successful Soap writer is the one who is able to let their strengths and personality as a writer shine through, while remaining true to voice of the show. If you have been given a trial script to read, try to use it only as a template for layout. Try not to be influenced by the style of that particular writer. Remember, the Producer is looking for someone to bring something new to the team, a fresh voice, fresh ideas.

The scene-by-scene breakdown

You are now in the same position as one of the regular scriptwriters when a new commission arrives. The first thing we have to do is to break the storyline down into a scene by scene structure. This process throws up various problems and this chapter will help you deal with them.

An example

Earlier on, you were shown an example of a storyline which was sent to me. I read all the storylines in the block, so I had an overview of what was happening before and after my episode and then set to work.

There are no hard and fast rules about how to write a scene breakdown. Some writers are minimalist, saying little more than who is in the scene and where it takes place. Others almost write the dialogue they are going to use in each scene, regarding this exercise as part of the process of writing the script. My approach falls between the two extremes. But before I show you an example, here are a few things to bear in mind:

The breakdown should serve as a working document for you and to let others know what you intend to do.

Don't be afraid to challenge the storyline. It is not set in stone. It is part of the evolution of the script. If there is something you disagree with, or if you can think of a better way of making a particular point, raise it at the commissioning conference. You may be over ruled, but equally you may be given the green light to go ahead. Remember, the script will have your name on it, so you need to be happy with what you're doing.

If you need anything clarifying, or help with any research, then speak out. (As mentioned earlier on Emmerdale and indeed The Archers, a detailed research document accompanies the storylines, but if you feel there is something that isn't covered, ask). Do, however, read the research document first. There is nothing more disheartening for the hard-working researcher to be asked a question about something already included in the booklet. It makes you look silly, too.

This is my breakdown for episode 5619 of *Emmerdale*:

SCENE BREAKDOWN EPISODE 5619

CHRIS THOMPSON

STUDIO SETS

Woolpack bar	(3)
Factory	(1)
Shop	(1)
Home Farm Office	(1)
Tall Trees	(1)

VILLAGE EXTERIORS

Main Street	(1)
Smithy Cottage	(1)
Factory	(2)
Village Hall	(1)

OTHER LOCATIONS

Ext Hotten Park	(6)

18 Scenes

1. I'm a bit concerned about Shadrach's line here and in 5618. In 5609, which I have just delivered, (and is therefore un-edited) I have people saying, in general gossip (it's the day after Aaron's revelation in court) that maybe he was saying he was gay in order to avoid prison. Someone also remarks on the fact that he went out with Holly. Further, I thought Jason, of long ago, was a gay Dingle. I also think that Shadrach saying maybe Aaron was trying to avoid prison here, dilutes the moment when Aaron says it, trying to save face. This doesn't leave Shadrach with much to say, unless we make him more obviously homophobic.

2. I assume the Community Service Officer is someone other than Danny, the probation officer. Can I invent someone and can s/he speak?

3. I've read the compliance directive in research documents and I see that in the story document both "queer" and "bender" are used. In order to reflect the attitudes that Wayne is expressing, we're going to have to use this type of language, or it will seem a bit anaemic. I'll use it sparingly but can I use those two words plus "puff"?

4. Is the project for which Declan is seeking planning permission, the one in the Home Farm grounds?

5. I'm a bit light on factory workers. (Chas and Gennie only).

6. When Aaron chats up the girls I don't want him to be too hopeless (after all he's done it before) but maybe they're out of his league. Wayne will still be motivated to give what he thinks is the real reason. (i.e., Aaron's sexuality).

7. I'm not convinced Chas would go and visit Aaron on community service. It's a good scene but surely she'd know how the other lads would react? Plus, she should be at work. I could play that she finds Aaron, on a break, away from the other lads. She goes for a chat, the others see her and it all kicks off. It makes her a bit more sussed.

8. This is very heavy on location.

SC 1 EXT SMITHY COTTAGE 08:30 DAY
AARON/ BETTY/PADDY/ RHONA

Paddy and Rhona try to be supportive as Aaron heads off to community service but he is clearly finding it tough.

    (Betty is storylined as making an acerbic remark. That's okay but I need to give her a reason to be there. Is she still cleaning the vets', or indeed anywhere?)

SC 2 INT TALL TREES 08:45 DAY
BOB/ MARLON

Bob expresses his anger and desperation at Viv's attitude and declares his determination to go on seeing the kids, whatever she says.

SC 3 EXT HOTTEN PARK 09:00 DAY
AARON/ WAYNE/ GARY DYSON (C.S.OFFICER)/ NS C.S.LADS

Aaron feels paranoid as he arrives, sensing that the other lads are talking about him as Gary explains the groups for the day's work.

(**Would the group be single sex or might girls be included, too?**)

SC 4 EXT FACTORY 10:30 DAY
GENNIE/ CHAS/ SHADRACH/ ZAK/ FAYE/ JAI/ NIKHIL

Gennie is despondent as Chas tells her how fed up Carl is over the hassle surrounding Aaron.

Chas confronts passing Shadrach (with Zak) about his attitude to Aaron the previous evening. Gennie confirms she noticed it too. Shadrach denies and slopes off.

Faye comes back from an errand to be greeted by Jai, who invites her to a business function that night. Coming out of the factory, to get the workers back, Nikhil senses he's interrupted something.

(**I've played the Jai-Nikhil-Faye beat alongside the others to avoid them feeling isolated. Please note my concerns re Shadrach at the top.**)

SC 5 INT HOME FARM OFFICE 10:50 DAY
DECLAN/ NICOLA/ NATASHA

Declan ribs Nicola for looking at a wedding brochure on the job. Noting his good mood, as Natasha walks in, Declan replies that he has a good feeling about things. His mood changes when he reads a letter from the council, explaining someone's voiced an objection to his application for planning permission.

SC 6 INT FACTORY 12:30 DAY
CHAS/ GENNIE/ FAYE/ JAI

As they break for lunch Faye persuades reluctant Gennie to go into the village but to try and steer clear of Viv. Gennie goes and flirtatious Jai persuades Faye to accompany him that evening.

SC 7 INT SHOP 12:40 DAY
VIV/ TERRY/ BETTY/ BRENDA

As Betty fishes for gossip, Terry tries to persuade Viv to give Bob a chance as she is the love of his life. Viv remains adamant, telling Terry that she can never forgive Bob and he will have to pay for it.

SC 8 INT THE WOOLPACK BAR 12:45 DAY
CHAS/ ZAK/ SHADRACH/ GENNIE/ LEYLA/ KATIE/ BOB/ MARLON/ MAISIE

Chas takes Shadrach to task over his attitude to Aaron. (**See my concern at the top.**)

Gennie tells Katie and Leyla about the playground incident yesterday and wonders if she should leave. Katie and Leyla try to dissuade her, giving her reasons to stay, starting with a girly night in.

SC 9 EXT HOTTEN PARK 13:00 DAY
AARON/WAYNE/GARY DYSON/N.S.C.S. LADS/LYNNE/ STACY

Aaron takes up Wayne's challenge and heads over to chat up two girls, masking his nerves.

SC 10 INT THE WOOLPACK BAR 13:10 DAY
NATASHA/ DECLAN/ FAYE/ JAI/ NIKHIL/ BOB/ MARLON/ CHAS/ GENNIE/ KATIE/ MAISIE/ BRENDA

Brenda arrives, anxious to tell Gennie about Viv's plans for divorce.

Natasha's chat to Declan about planning is spoiled when Faye arrives with Jai and Nikhil. Declan goes to talk to Jai, Nikhil to Maisie and Natasha finds herself alone with Faye. She makes her excuses to Declan and leaves. Declan clocks the tension between Faye and Natasha.

SC 11 EXT HOTTEN PARK 13:05 DAY
AARON/ WAYNE/ N.S.C.S.LADS/ LYNNE/ STACEY

Aaron fails to chat up Lynne and Stacey, who leave. His macho front to the lads is punctured by Wayne, who tells him he screwed up because he's gay; he saw it in the paper. Aaron is utterly thrown.

END OF PART ONE.

SC 12 INT THE WOOLPACK BAR 13:10 DAY
BRENDA/ GENNIE/ LEYLA/ KATIE/ MAISIE/ RHONA/ PADDY

Brenda tells Gennie about Viv's intention to divorce Bob. Gennie is devastated and Brenda unsympathetic. Leyla and Katie offer support.
(I'll give Rhona and Paddy a second beat here).

SC 13 EXT HOTTEN PARK 13:15 DAY
AARON/ WAYNE/ N.S.C.S.LADS/ GARY DYSON

As Gary chivvies the lads back to work Aaron vehemently denies being gay, saying he only said he was to avoid being sent down. Aaron feels ashamed of himself as the lads seemingly buy it.

SC 14 EXT VILLAGE HALL 15:30 DAY
BOB/ TERRY/ JIMMY

Bob is distraught as he tells Jimmy and Terry that he can't see the twins as **Viv has taken him off the carers' list.** (I was surprised by this and haven't seen the research document yet) Terry realises he'll have to have it out with Viv.

SC 15 EXT HOTTEN PARK 16:30 DAY
AARON/ WAYNE/ NS C.S. LADS/ GARY DYSON/ CHAS

Chas's visit serves to embarrass Aaron hugely.
(See my note at the top—I'm not sure Chas would do this so have suggested an alternative choreography.)

SC 16 EXT FACTORY 17:00 DAY
DECLAN/ FAYE/ JAI

Declan greets Faye and Jai outside the factory and apologises for putting her in an awkward position earlier.

Declan hopes things might get easier between them, as he and Jai are good mates and would be nice to feel they could all go out sometime. Exchanging a charged look with Faye, Jai is already two steps in front of Declan. Playing it cool, Faye casually agrees it might be possible, one day.

(I need some clarification. Is Declan suggesting the four of them go out? And what does "Jai is already two steps ahead of Declan" mean?)

SC 17 EXT MAIN STREET 17:05 DAY
JIMMY/ BOB/ VIV/ NICOLA/ CATHY/ HEATH

Jimmy is trying to persuade Bob to come for a drink and witnesses a bitter and angry exchange between Bob and Viv, with Bob expressing his determination to fight any petition for divorce.

(I'll give Nicola a second beat here).

SC 18 EXT HOTTEN PARK 17:10 DAY
AARON/ WAYNE

Filled with self-loathing, Aaron finds himself locked in the shed, subjected to homophobic abuse and being bullied for the first time in his life. He is rocked by the depth of his own vulnerability.

What do you notice?

There are 18 scenes. There is no hard and fast rule about how many scenes an episode should contain. On *Emmerdale* it is usually between 18 and 24. This particular episode was the first of two shown on the same evening, one at 7o'clock, the other at 8. Watch episodes of *Eastenders*, *Coronation Street* and *Hollyoaks* and see how the scene count compares.

On the front page, I indicate how many scenes are based in studio and how many are on location. The balance between studio and location should normally be about 60–40 in favour of Studio. You'll notice that two thirds of this episode takes place on location. This is primarily because the A story is Aaron doing his community service, which had to be filmed on location. However, the balance can be evened out in the whole block, so one person's studio usage buys location usage somewhere else. Without a proper balance, it is impossible to schedule the programme, as separate crews need to be working simultaneously.

Hotten is the fictional market town near to *Emmerdale*. Hotten is in fact filmed in Otley, in Wharfedale. Soaps strangely use a mixture of fictional and real names. Thus characters who inhabit *Emmerdale*, *Weatherfield* or *Walford*, talk about (and go to or are part of) Leeds, Manchester and London.

There used to be a convention that an episode of Soap should begin at breakfast and end at night, reflecting the shape of a day in the life of the characters. This episode is in fact the first of two continuous ones, ending late at night. Thus I chose to begin it in the morning and close it around tea time, allowing the second episode to take place through the evening. The timings should suit the way you want to shape the episode. Some may start at lunchtime; others may play entirely through the evening and into the night. This flexibility is healthy: I once watched an episode of a Soap (which shall be nameless) which began with six separate breakfast scenes. This seemed like taking the convention a tad too far and was boringly repetitive. (You need to bear in mind, too, the balance between daytime and night time. Episodes shot in the winter months will inevitably involve night time shoots, so your timing of scenes should reflect this).

You need not follow the storyline to the letter. If it reads "X meets Y in the cafe and tells him the deal is off", you do not have to use the cafe, if it doesn't suit your purposes. The important detail is the interaction between the characters.

You should, equally, not be wedded to the words of the document. You'll have noticed in my scene breakdown that I reduced the beats in most cases from a paragraph to a couple of sentences and tried to use my own language to express the same thoughts and ideas. This is an important step in moving from the story document to the first draft, towards making the episode your own. Some writers go further, expressing the content of a scene in one sentence. Others will write more than is in the document, including stage directions and snippets of dialogue. In effect, they are beginning the script writing process. A third way is simply to cut and paste the document, but in my view, this is the least satisfactory method. It's quick, to be sure and means you deliver your breakdown with a minimum of fuss, but it keeps you wedded to the document and implies there is nothing you wish to change.

You'll notice that I have looked for opportunities to cross different story strands within the same scene. Thus, scene 4, in the Factory and scene 8 and 10, in the pub, contain elements of different stories. It is important to do this, to show how lives interact and to prevent the episode appearing like a series of isolated bubbles. It was particularly relevant in this episode, where the Aaron strand took place away from the village, and was impossible to cross with any other stories. You may be told that certain characters cannot cross in certain episodes, due to schedule constraints, and that should be addressed at this stage.

Care has to be taken in finding a strong scene to lead into the advertising break. This is obviously not an issue on BBC programmes, but on the commercial network, the "Ad Tag" is the mini-hook that you hope will bring the audience back after the break.

You need to respect the realities of the working day. Soaps are rooted in the everyday lives of their characters and they can't be mooching around the pub all day long. This is another advantage of the communal sets, where people can meet over a coffee, a pint, buying a loaf of bread, having their hair done or doing a load of washing in the laundrette. But it should happen realistically, when people cross, at lunchtime, before or after work. The advantage of a set like *Underworld* in *Coronation Street* is that it is a workplace set but is also communal, given the range of people who interact there. That is why specific times are used in Soaps. So, at the top of the scene it might say INT WOOLPACK 13:00 DAY or EXT MAIN. STREET 22:00 NIGHT. In the first instance, 13:00 is a time when people might realistically be in the pub having lunch. When planning an episode the writer needs to place the action at specific times, so the drama will have the feel of a real day. The second example, which takes place at 22:00 NIGHT will obviously entail a night time shoot, as it's an exterior location. This will have implications when the filming schedule is being drawn up.

You should be left with an outline which fits the rhythms and realities of the community. You should be aware of characters' moments through the day, so that it feels real and organic. If it doesn't, it will feel unrealistic and you can bet the audience will notice.

What has been questioned?

I have already suggested that you have the confidence to challenge the storyline. There were a number of issues I wished to raise in this episode. I have listed my questions at the top of the document and others are highlighted in bold. Let's look at the things I am concerned about.

1. My first question concerns Shadrach's attitude towards Aaron's sexuality. We have to be realistic and confront the fact that homophobia exists. In fact, the sequence in the park is all about Aaron's first encounter with these attitudes and he finds it difficult. He has always cultivated the image of a hard man and the reason he is doing community service at all is because he hit someone he was attracted to, in denial of his true feelings. But Shadrach is (or was at that time) one of our regular characters. To give a well-liked and generally benign, regular character illiberal attitudes can alienate the audience. This happened on *The Archers*, when a casually racist remark in the mouth of a long-standing character, tainted the public's view of her for a long time.

2. This may seem a trivial question, but actors who speak cost more money than ones who don't. So by wishing to introduce such a character, I am increasing the budget. (You'll notice how many NSEs—non speaking extras—say thank you to a shopkeeper or barman without uttering a word.)

3. This relates to my first question. Compliance, which I discuss later, governs what we can say and at what time. If the programme was going out after 9 o'clock, this wouldn't be such an issue, but at 7, it is.

4. This is seeking clarification of a detail in the story document.

5. Again, this may seem trivial, but the factory is supposed to be a busy place of work and it would look silly if only two characters were there. There is, however, a social area built into that set, where two or three characters can meet without having to see the shop floor.

6. This highlights an important point when I come to write the script. Aaron has had relationships with girls before, so I didn't want him to be too inept, in spite of his inner conflict.

7. I raised this here but was asked to write in her visit and see how it played. I did, but it was patently not right, so it was dropped at a later draft. I didn't say "I told you so"!

8. This may seem like stating the obvious, but I wanted to raise it at this early stage. (It doesn't, however, prevent one being asked to move some scenes into studio at a later stage in the process.)

I have also raised a number of issues in bold next to various scenes:

In scene 1, I want to make sure that Betty has a reason to be there. It relates to the point I made about the episode reflecting the realities of the working day.

In scene 3, I discovered that girls could be in the group, which added to the realism of the situation.

Scene 4 explains my reasons for staging the scene this way.

Scene 16 seeks clarification of a storyline beat that didn't seem clear.

Now, this may seem like a lot of questions, but it is important to ask them at this stage. If changes are agreed, to Shadrach's attitude for instance, it will affect the way other writers write him later in the block.

Respect the storyline but don't be a slave to it. It has to work as a piece of drama, so don't be afraid to move things around and ask for changes if you think it will improve the script. Remember, nothing is set in stone at this stage and what eventually appears on screen comes at the end of a long, constantly evolving process.

7 Script layout

An overview

This chapter will show a sample Soap script layout. It is different from a film script and, say, an hour long TV drama script. They are all, however, essentially variations on a theme. By looking at the sample layout, you will get some insight into the technical issues involved in writing for television.

But first, what is a scene?

In longer, free standing TV drama, writers are encouraged to think in terms of Acts; that is, arranging clusters of scenes into larger groups, as you would in a stage play, or a film.

In Soap, however, episodes are structured, as you'll see, in scenes. The purpose of a scene is to move the story along and/or to develop character. Each scene should have a purpose. This doesn't mean that every scene should be plot driven. It may be two or three characters talking, apparently inconsequentially, but it should develop our understanding of those characters and what they are thinking and feeling. (This will be developed in a later chapter.)

An extract

Here are scenes 1 and 2 of the *Emmerdale* episode we have been considering, as it appeared in the first draft:

LOC   AARON/PADDY/BETTY/RHONA
SC 1 EXT SMITHY COTTAGE 08:30 DAY

PADDY WALKS OUT OF SMITHY COTTAGE WITH AARON, WHO IS DOWNBEAT AS HE HEADS TO

Margin Note
As we mentioned earlier, a tv script is usually set only on the right hand side. This leaves the left hand side for actors and technicians to add notes.

THE BUS STOP TO ATTEND COMMUNITY SERVICE. RHONA WALKS FROM THE SHOP, WITH BETTY.

PADDY :   Are you sure you don't want a lift?

AARON: Positive.

PADDY :   It's no trouble. (TO RHONA) You can start surgery, can't you, if I take Aaron in …

RHONA: Sure.

AARON: I said no.

PADDY :   I know but …

AARON: But what?

PADDY :   I'm trying to help.

AARON: By dropping me off like some little kid?

BETTY :   Don't take it out on Paddy. You should be thankful you're not behind bars.

AARON: Who asked you?

PADDY :   Did you want something, Betty?

BETTY :   I told Edna I'd pick up Tootsie's tablets.

RHONA: So let's go and get them, shall we?

RHONA POINTS RELUCTANT BETTY TOWARDS THE SURGERY.

RHONA: (JOLLY) You never know you might make a few mates …

AARON GLARES STONILY AT RHONA, WHO WISHES SHE'D SAID NOTHING.

RHONA: Then again …

RHONA FOLLOWS BETTY. AARON GOES FOR THE BUS LEAVING PADDY CONCERNED FOR HIM.
   CUT TO:

STUDIO   BOB/MARLON
SC 2 INT TALL TREES 08:35 DAY

MARLON COMES INTO THE KITCHEN TO MAKE COFFEE. HE FINDS BOB, UNSHAVEN, IN HIS PYJAMAS, AT THE TABLE, WHICH IS COVERED IN SCRAPS OF PAPER WITH WRITING ON THEM.

MARLON	:	What's all this?
BOB	:	A soul in turmoil …
MARLON	:	That's why you got up in the middle of the night …
BOB	:	Sorry, but my head was full of things I want to say to Viv. And I wanted to write them all down. In case I forgot them.

MARLON PICKS UP A SHEET AT RANDOM.

MARLON	:	(READS) "Yesterday?"
BOB	:	That's like a bullet point. This time yesterday I thought we could patch things up. A few hours later she wanted a divorce and the kids and she doesn't even want me to see them.
MARLON	:	She can't stop you, can she?

BOB HANDS MARLON A PIECE OF PAPER. IT READS "YOU CAN'T STOP ME."

BOB	:	I know I started all this. I made a mistake. But we could've come through it. Only Viv won't let it rest.
MARLON	:	You've had your problems before …
BOB	:	I know, but Viv won't listen. She can't forgive and she won't forget. You'd think she never loved me …

BOB PUTS HIS HEAD IN HIS HANDS. UNSEEN, MARLON PICKS UP ANOTHER PIECE OF PAPER, THE WRITING SMUDGED. WE SEE IT READS "I CAN'T STOP CRYING." MARLON'S HEART GOES OUT TO BOB.

CUT TO:

Before we look at the format and technical aspects of the layout, let's consider the content. The episode opens outside, at the top of Main Street, next to Smithy Cottage where Paddy, the vet, lives and has his surgery. By opening an episode outside, in the village or at one of our regular locations, Butler's Farm or Home Farm, we welcome the audience back to the world of *Emmerdale* and village and introduce them to one or more of the stories we'll be telling. We also pick up from where we left our key characters at the end of the previous episode.

Thus Aaron sets out for his first day on community service. He is dreading it, but refuses help from Paddy. Paddy has taken him in and offered him support throughout his struggle with his sexuality. However, Aaron remains stubbornly determined to go alone. Betty, with a reason to be there (see my question in the breakdown) is tactless, as is Rhona, although their motives are different. Ideally, I would have liked to cross this with another story strand, but it didn't prove possible. But we send Aaron off to Hotten, wondering what he'll encounter. (By the time we get to the third draft, this scene had changed, with Betty gone, replaced by Aaron's friend, Adam).

In scene two, we see Bob, separated from his wife Viv, following an ill-advised fling and staying with Marlon. He has been up most of the night writing down things he wants to say to Viv. He is desperately worried that he'll lose her and their two children, Heath and Cathy. Marlon is unable to console him.

We have introduced the two main story strands of the episode.

So much for content …

You'll see that the script occupies the right half of the page, only. This allows the left half to be used by the actor, for making notes; by the director, planning the way he or she wishes to shoot the scene and by the people responsible for make-up, lighting, costume, props and so on. It's a working space, and helps them ensure continuity.

At the top of the page you see the abbreviation **LOC** which of course is short for LOCATION. **STUDIO** is self-explanatory.

There follows a list of the characters in that scene. This is called the **STRAP LINE.**

We then see the number of the scene, where it takes place and the exact time of day or night. **SC 1 EXT SMITHY COTTAGE 08:30 DAY** Remember this detail is important to the schedulers when they work out the details of the shoot. Four episodes will normally be shot in tandem so this is a complex and vital process.

EXT is short for Exterior, **INT** for Interior.

The script itself contains **DIALOGUE** and **STAGE DIRECTIONS**. The dialogue is self-explanatory. All the instructions in **UPPER CASE LETTERS** are, quaintly, called Stage Directions.

They serve two purposes: to choreograph the action, indicating where characters move, when they leave the scene or arrive. This will obviously be developed by the director, who has the job of making the whole thing work.

So at the top of scene one, we establish where the characters are coming from, physically and also Aaron's mood. Later on, Aaron doesn't respond to Rhona verbally, but gives her a stony look. It is important to remember that you're working in a visual medium and Stage Directions also serve to give the actor guidance on their feelings, reactions, or the emotion required in delivering a particular piece of dialogue, or they can take the place of dialogue. Writers vary in how prescriptive they are. I tend towards the minimalist, allowing actors and directors to bring their own ideas and believing that if the dialogue is right then the emotion should be clear. (It doesn't always happen the way I intend, but it can be better and bring something I hadn't considered to the playing of the scene.) However, we see that apart from Aaron being downbeat, Rhona tries to be jolly and we close on Paddy's concern. Another commonly used Stage Direction is (BEAT) which is often inserted in the middle of a speech. It is a mini pause, a single heartbeat, or breathing space, if you like. It can be used where a character is having difficulty saying something, struggling with their emotions, or it can allow them to change tack.

In the second scene, Bob's dishevelled appearance hints at his state of mind and at the end he puts his head in his hands. And by Marlon reading one of Bob's random notes, we get an insight into Bob's feelings, without the use of dialogue.

Each scene ends with the words **CUT TO:** This is the link to the next scene. You will often go out on what is called a **REACTION SHOT** i.e., you look at a particular character and indicate a specific emotion you want them to convey. Alternatively, you may go out on an action.

In film and in other TV drama, you will often see what is known as a **JUMP CUT**. This is where you go out of one scene, with a character leaving his home and in the next scene you see him entering an office building. In other words, we jump time. In Soap we don't do this, there would have to be a scene in between, to account for the missing time. It's a fairly rigid convention, although it can be frustrating.

A task

Practice using this format. Choose one of the scenes from the breakdown or put together a group of characters from another Soap and write a short scene for them. The formats for different shows may vary slightly, but get used to telling a story not only through dialogue, but using stage directions in the way I've indicated.

Getting started

By now, you should understand the programmes and the way they are made. You have been shown how stories make their way on to the screen, how individual episodes are structured from storyline documents and how your script should be set out on the page. This chapter will show you how to present your script in the right way, showing your understanding of the genre, helping to persuade a producer to offer you a chance.

A sobering thought

There are probably fewer than one hundred and fifty people writing Soap in the UK, if you consider the relative size of the teams producing them. There are no doubt thousands more who would give anything for the chance to join them. No formal qualifications are required: as I pointed out before, writers come from all backgrounds: some left school early, had young families, did a variety of jobs before discovering what they really wanted to do was write. Others did media related courses and were dead set on a career in TV from the word go. The only qualification required is the ability to write. When a Producer reads your script, he or she isn't remotely interested in where you went to school or university. They want to know if you can write.

The goal

The person reading your trial script will have read hundreds, possibly thousands of scripts of their show, from writers past and present and from people who aspire to join the team. You have to make yours stand out from the crowd, showing you understand the programme and its conventions but bringing something new.

Make it leap from the page

This is a phrase often used by producers and script editors. It means a script (and by extension a writer) has that X factor, that touch of individuality and originality which makes them want to meet you and employ you. We often talk about novels we've enjoyed as "page turners". Your script should have that quality. You achieve it by the way you handle dialogue, your understanding of character, the way you come at a story, finding an original way to tell it.

A check list

> *Before writing, you will take the storyline and break it down into individual scenes.*
> *Your episode will have 18–24 scenes.*
> *You know how to set your script out, on the page.*
> *You have watched the show and are familiar with the characters and its style.*

You're almost ready to start, but you need one final bit of information, and that involves the **LENGTH** of your episode.

Each time you deliver a draft script, it will be timed, to see how close it is to the exact running time required. Dialogue will be read out loud and allowance made for action sequences involving no dialogue. By the time the episode is recorded and delivered to the Network for transmission, it will be timed to the second. If at that stage it over runs, then recorded material will have to be cut in the editing process. Again, this is taken for granted in the world of film. In the cost conscious world of popular drama, it's seen as a waste of time and money.

You would be forgiven for thinking that an episode of a Soap is 30 minutes long. Well, not exactly. If it is on BBC, like *Eastenders*, it will be 30 minutes, minus the opening title sequence and the closing credits. On ITV, a further reduction is made because of the advertising break in the middle. Thus, on *Emmerdale*, for example, the actual script length is closer to 24 minutes. Now, you won't be expected to nail the timing exactly with your trial script, but if you can get somewhere near, then it shows you have thought about that aspect of the programme. It gives them another reason to employ you.

Some writers read their scripts aloud before submitting them. I tend to use the word count on my computer. I aim to deliver a script of approximately 4800 words (including stage directions, scene headings and strap lines). This usually comes out between 60 and 68 pages, using the format I have illustrated. The length will vary according to the nature of a particular episode and the style of individual writers. Some episodes are very heavy on dialogue; others may contain a lot of action. I aim to deliver about 1 to 2 minutes over, at each edit, leaving a bit of room for trims.

A tip

Try not to deliver under length. It is easier to trim scripts than to add on at a later stage. I have had phone calls at an advanced stage of recording, telling me an episode is running two minutes under, when there are only three scenes left to shoot in the schedule, involving four characters in prescribed locations. And the extra time has to be found in those scenes. It can be difficult to write fresh, sparkling dialogue and to avoid padding. You'd be amazed how quickly actors devour dialogue, even in scenes which seem to be played slowly. So if you err, err on the side of writing too much, not too little. It's better for your blood pressure.

Challenge the storyline

You know how a storyline is put together and you have seen an example of one. It will have been written by people who may aspire to be scriptwriters and who will certainly have the ability to write and they will have put their mark on it, quite rightly. You have to make it your own.

Ask yourself the following questions:

> *Is this the best way to tell these particular stories?*
>
> *Are there any missing beats, extra moments that would make it work better?*
>
> *Do I want to drop any beats, as they seem redundant or repetitive?*
>
> *Are there any characters I would like to drop or add?*
>
> *Do I have a moment that will make a strong Ad Tag? If I have more than one, which one should I choose?*
>
> *Is the end of episode tag strong enough? Is there a better one to be had?*
>
> *As I put together the scene-by-scene breakdown, do the various story strands hang together as a workable episode?*
>
> *Can I cross different strands to give texture to the episode?*
>
> *What times of day do I begin and end my episode?*

As a member of the writing team, you would be able to ask these questions at commissioning. On your own, faced with a trial script, you will have to make your own decisions.

Two more tips

Be wary of changing the end of episode tag. The storyline team will have looked across a block of 24 episodes when deciding on the tags, with the aim of leading on to the next episode in a dynamic way and not repeating a similar beat in another episode. If you DO decide to change it, make sure it comes from one of the major strands.

Avoid using characters only once in scripts. It looks odd and they feel peripheral to the episode. If a character appears only once in the storyline document, find another place to put her or him. Either that, or lose them. A writer on the team would ask this at commissioning conference. It may be that a character hasn't been seem much on screen in recent episodes, so the producer will be keen to keep them in. In that case, you have to find them something meaningful to do or say, hopefully within the context of an ongoing story.

A stories and B, C and D stories

When you are structuring your episode, you need to bear in mind the weight given to the various story strands in your storyline document. Clearly, the A strand is going to form the backbone of your script. It should feature throughout your episode and be a significant element of **at least** three scenes either side of the Ad Break. It will almost certainly form the end of episode hook and possibly the Ad Tag as well, although this is not compulsory. There may be another story which you may want to play around the commercial break.

(Again, this will not be an issue if writing for the BBC, but making sure your main story stand is given sufficient weight, will be equally important.)

It is a good idea to separate out the elements of your A strand before arranging the other stories around it. When doing this, bear in mind that one paragraph in the storyline document does not necessarily equate to one scene. You may want to divide the elements of a paragraph, or combine two of them. What is essential is that each scene should move the story along. We should be in a different place by the end of each scene, wondering what is going to happen next.

When you consider the other story strands in your episode, try to play some of them alongside other strands. In television, a C story in a stand-alone scene is likely to look pretty thin.

Intercutting

Look for opportunities to make the structure part of the storytelling. The sequence of scenes can in itself reinforce the dramatic point you are trying to make. Let me give an example from the episode we have been looking at:

LOC   BOB/ TERRY/ JIMMY/ NICOLA/ TJ/ Extras
SC 14 EXT VILLAGE HALL 15:30 DAY

JIMMY WALKS WITH NICOLA FROM THE POST OFFICE, TO HER CAR OPPOSITE THE VILLAGE HALL WHERE A GROUP OF PARENTS WAIT FOR NURSERY TO END.

JIMMY :	Have you got time to see Angel?
NICOLA:	I can't go over there. They're all looking at me.
JIMMY :	No, they're not.

IN FACT, ONE OR TWO ARE.

NICOLA:	I said I'd get straight back. Declan's probably got a stop watch on me.
JIMMY :	I'll hold your hand.

EDNA APPROACHES FROM THE CHURCH.

EDNA :	I've been thinking about your flowers. And I might just be able to make the changes you want.
JIMMY :	What changes?
NICOLA:	I'll tell you later.
EDNA :	I've asked Eve to help me. She wasn't very keen but she's got nothing better to do. So we're going into town this afternoon.
NICOLA:	I'm really grateful.
EDNA :	I'll be in touch later.

EDNA GOES.

JIMMY :	You sure you won't come with me?
NICOLA:	I can't take any liberties.

SHE GETS IN HER CAR AND DRIVES AWAY. JIMMY GOES TO JOIN THE PARENTS AS TERRY PULLS UP, WITH TJ, IN HIS CAR. HE SEES BOB, WALKING OUT OF THE VILLAGE HALL, LOOKING TERRIBLE, AND GOES ACROSS.

JIMMY :	You look terrible …
BOB :	I've been talking to Mrs Cowling.
JIMMY :	Nothing's happened to the twins?

TERRY ARRIVES.

BOB	:	Not how you mean, no. I told her I'd be picking them up today but she said I can't. Viv's taken me off the carers' list. I'm their dad. I didn't even know I was on a list.
TERRY	:	Do you want me to have a word?
BOB	:	My problem. I've got to sort it.

BOB IS IN BITS.
    CUT TO:

LOC   CHAS/ AARON/ WAYNE/ GARY/ Community Payback Team
SC 15 EXT HOTTEN PARK 16:30 DAY

WAYNE AND AARON ARE HOLDING A FENCE POST BETWEEN THEM, CLOSE TO THE EDGE OF THE LAKE.

WAYNE	:	So have you got a bird, or haven't you?
AARON	:	I told you …
WAYNE	:	You didn't tell me anything …
AARON	:	I told you, it's nowt to do with you …
WAYNE	:	If you had, you'd say so, wouldn't you?
AARON	:	All right, I have, satisfied?
WAYNE	:	I don't believe you, gay boy …

WITH A SUDDEN SHARP MOVEMENT, WAYNE PUSHES HARD ON THE FENCE POST. AARON LOSES HIS BALANCE, STUMBLES BACKWARDS AND FALLS INTO THE POND.
    WAYNE LAUGHS AS AARON FLOUNDERS IN THE SHALLOW WATER, BEFORE CLIMBING OUT, DRIPPING WET. HE WALKS TOWARDS WAYNE.

| WAYNE | : | Have a nice swim? |

WE CLOSE ON AARON, FURIOUS.
    CUT TO:

STUDIO

BOB/ VIV/ BRENDA/ Cathy/ Heath
SC 16 INT CAFE 16:32 DAY

BOB ARRIVES, DETERMINED AND TACKLES BRENDA, BEHIND THE COUNTER.

BOB	:	I want to speak to Viv. Where is she?
BRENDA:		She's busy.
BOB	:	She's not in the shop.
BRENDA:		I know that.
BOB	:	So where is she?
BRENDA:		Don't take that tone with me.
BOB	:	I'll take whatever tone I like. I want to see my wife.

VIV APPEARS FROM THE FLAT, WITH HEATH AND CATHY.

VIV	:	But she doesn't want to see you.
BOB	:	(TO BRENDA) You knew she was up there, didn't you?
BRENDA:		I didn't think you'd want to see him.
VIV	:	I don't.
BOB	:	That's too bad, because we've got things to sort out.
VIV	:	I'm not interested. And anyway, I'm running late …
BOB	:	Late for what? (NO REPLY) Where are you going?
VIV	:	If you must know, I'm going to see my solicitor.
BOB	:	About a divorce?
VIV	:	You'll get a letter, in due course.
BOB	:	You can't wait, can you?
VIV	:	No, I can't. The sooner I'm free from you, the better.

BOB LOOKS HURT.

BOB	:	Alright, if that's what you want, go and see your precious solicitor. (BEAT) But there's no need to trail those two into town. I'll look after them till you get back.

VIV :	Oh no, you won't. I told them to tell you at nursery …
BOB:	Yeah, they did: something about a carers' list. That's why I'm here. You're not seriously trying to stop me seeing my own kids?
VIV :	Yes, I am. And I'm entitled to do it.
BOB:	Come on, Viv. Surely I can spend a couple of hours with them …
VIV :	I don't want you spending a couple of minutes with them. I'm not just going to talk about divorce. I want sole custody. I don't want you anywhere near them, ever.

BOB IS POLEAXED.

These are three scenes which come towards the end of the episode. In the first half of an episode, the various story strands are set up and established, but as the episode moves towards it close, the focus is on the main story strands. Thus in scene 14, after dealing with Nicola's approaching wedding, Bob takes centre stage as he discovers that he is being prevented from seeing his children. We then cut to Aaron at the end of his day from hell, being pushed into the lake and humiliated. From there, we go back to Bob confronting Viv, who delivers her hammer blow, refusing to offer Bob any comfort.

In fact, in the final edit, it was decided to go with this scene as the end of episode. As I indicated earlier, this is unusual, but we felt it was easier to pick up on the row between Viv and Bob and allow time to have moved on before coming back to the lake, as Aaron confronted his tormentor, in scene two of the next episode. The scenes build a momentum, which drives us to the end of the episode and lead us to look forward to the next. So we wonder what Bob will do and, more immediately, how Aaron is going to react.

In another episode, we might have two characters anxiously discussing the behaviour of their daughter. We could cut from them to the daughter; doing the exact thing they fear the most: stealing, drinking, taking drugs, whatever.

A good structure gives the episode a sense of cohesion and progression. Don't chuck scenes together without thought. Think of the process as a kind of choreography.

(If you are eagle-eyed, you will have noticed that the storyline document has Aaron being locked in a shed, whereas here he is pushed into the lake. This change came about as the result of the editing process, as the three drafts evolved. There will be much more of this, later.)

Communal sets

This is where communal sets and locations come into their own. I have mentioned already the significance of *Main Street* in *Emmerdale*, *Albert Square* in *Eastenders* and *Coronation Street* itself. The three iconic pubs, the *Rover's Return*, the *Queen Vic* and the *Woolpack* have similar importance. These are the places where people interact, where their lives cross, where casual conversations and major confrontations take place.

They also serve a more prosaic purpose. They allow the writer to put different groups of characters together in a natural, organic way. In the next chapter, I shall give an example of how to structure and write such a scene, but when you are plotting out an episode, be alive to their potential, and that of the other communal spaces and places. If you don't use them, then the chances are, as part of the editing process, you will be asked to move some scenes into them. If story strands never cross, the episode will feel like a series of self-contained story bubbles.

Two-handers

At the other end of the scale, is the two-handed scene, where two characters talk, argue, fight, love and hate each other. They are important, because we all have moments alone with our partners, workmates, friends and enemies. They can be very, very powerful.

A few years ago, I wrote two-handed episode of *Emmerdale* featuring Ashley Thomas, the vicar, and his first wife, Bernice. It charted the breakdown of their marriage and was told in real time—30 minutes action told in 30 minutes (or, as you'll recall, 24). It was wonderful to write and worked well. *Eastenders* memorably gave Dot Cotton a one-woman episode, but such occasions are rare.

If you have too many two-handers in an episode it can seem too samey, too predictable. It can lack the spark and vitality that multi-strand scenes can have. Ideally an episode will be a mixture of two-handers, of bustling communal scenes, of dialogue and action.

Variety is all.

9 The writing process

An overview

You should now have the structure of your episode in place and have decided what, if any changes you intend to make to the storyline. You have a mixture of location and studio based scenes organised in an effective structure. Now you have to hit those keys, move characters around and put words in their mouths. This is what you've been waiting to do. This chapter aims to help you give your script that extra something.

Don't be a slave to the storyline—the sequel

I've already suggested that you challenge the content of the storyline, looking for ways in which it might be improved. And in the chapter on writing a scene breakdown, I encouraged you to start moving away from the language of the storyline, looking to express the ideas in your own words. This is even more important when it comes to writing the script. Don't whatever you do, reproduce chunks of the storyline document and put them in the mouths of the characters. The story document is a starting point, not the finished article. The breakdown gives you the opportunity to use your own language; when it comes to the script, you are expressing ideas through the words of the characters, and that should be your aim.

My first TV job was writing on the daytime Soap, *Families*, made by Granada and devised by Kay Mellor. It ran from 1990–1993. I was anxious to please and in the early days stuck far too close to the actual language of the document. It took a friendly hint from the Producer to give me the confidence to move away from it. She could equally have given me the sack.

The purpose of the scene

You should approach each scene like a miniature play. It should have a specific purpose. It may be to pass on a piece of information from one character to another, to allow a character to express their feelings or opinions, to bring characters together or drive them apart, to reveal an important plot detail. At the other end of the scale, it could be a set-piece scene, like a wedding, a funeral, a murder or the beginning of an affair. (These events will probably stretch over several scenes or even an episode—more on this later.) It should begin organically and end in a way that leads us forward, leaving the audience in expectation as to what might happen next.

The shape of the scene

You may recall *Acorn Antiques*, Victoria Wood's brilliant spoof of Soap Opera, inspired by *Crossroads* and its legendary wobbly sets. Scenes often began with characters standing still, frozen, looking anxiously towards the camera waiting for the Assistant Director to shout "action". It was a master class in how not to write, act or direct Soap, or for that matter any drama. Not every scene can have people coming and going, some may involve two characters in the middle of a conversation, but a scene should have a dynamic, some movement, be it physical or emotional. At the other end of the spectrum, not every scene should begin with characters saying "hi" or "hello", nor end with them saying "goodbye." You need to find ways to inject some movement into your scenes, not have them frozen in time or space.

Different agendas

Different characters will have different agendas in the same scene. This doesn't mean every scene will contain an argument, although some will, and conflict is at the heart of drama. Writing scenes in this way, gives them depth and complexity and allows the audience to enjoy seeing and decoding the varying reactions and opinions of the protagonists.

To illustrate this point, let's consider another scene from the *Emmerdale* episode we've been looking at. Nobody dies, throws a mug at the wall, or hits anyone else, it is, in a way a bread and butter scene, but it will show how one scene does the three things I have just mentioned.

By way of background: the scene takes place at the Sharma factory, owned and run by the brothers Nikhil and Jai. Chas (short for Chastity) and Gennie work there and are half-sisters. Gennie has recently been dumped by her long term boyfriend Jamie, who has started a new life in Newquay without her. Chas, Aaron's mother, lives with Carl, but is worried about his antipathy towards Aaron. She's worried it is homophobia, but he claims he never liked him, even before he came out. Both Chas and Gennie are disappointed in their father, Shadrach, who really does have a problem with Aaron's sexuality. They are interrupted by first Jai and then Nikhil. The two women go back to work and Jai teases Nikhil about Maisie, who has called with a message for Nikhil. Nikhil fancies Maisie, who seems to like him in return, but Nikhil is slow to do anything about it (for reasons we discover later).

**STUDIO   GENNIE/ CHAS/ SHADRACH/ JAI/
NIKHIL/ Extras
SC 4 INT FACTORY 10:30 DAY**

GENNIE AND CHAS ARE ON A BREAK IN THE LOCKER ROOM.

CHAS :	So how's it going then, first day back?
GENNIE:	It's better than queuing up at the job centre. But I keep hearing seagulls and waves crashing on the beach and thinking about Newquay …
CHAS :	You'd have hated it. You'd have spent every day gazing at fit-looking surfers. You'd have soon got fed up …
GENNIE:	It wouldn't be surfers I'd be gazing at.

CHAS	:	I reckon we're both mugs. Life'd be a lot simpler without fellers …
GENNIE:		It's easy for you to say, you've got Carl.
CHAS	:	And he's doing my head in.
GENNIE:		Have you had a row? Is that why he wasn't there last night?
CHAS	:	He said he didn't fancy it. (BEAT) But it could've been 'cos of Aaron. I thought he'd started to accept him. I don't know …

JAI COMES IN FOR A COFFEE.

GENNIE:		It was bad enough listening to dad going on.
CHAS	:	I could've throttled him. Aaron's his grandson. You'd think he'd have some sympathy for him.
JAI	:	Families, eh?

NIKHIL ARRIVES.

| NIKHIL: | | Are you talking about me? |
| CHAS | : | No, he's being nosy. |

CHAS AND GENNIE GO BACK TO THE FACTORY.

JAI	:	Paranoid, or what?
NIKHIL:		I know you; you're as big a gossip as that lot out there.
JAI	:	Then give me something to gossip about.
NIKHIL:		Sorry to disappoint you.
JAI	:	I wouldn't be too sure. Things might be looking up …
NIKHIL:		How do you mean?
JAI	:	Maisie rang this morning, said to tell you she was working this lunchtime. Hoped you'd call in to nibble on a cheese butty …
NIKHIL:		She said that?
JAI	:	Obviously she didn't say butty, 'cos she's posh.

JAI GRINS.

NIKHIL:	You're lying.
JAI :	Had you going though, didn't I? I bet your little heart was pounding there for a minute.
NIKHIL:	You really are juvenile …
JAI :	You're the one who gazes at her behind the bar like a love sick poodle.
NIKHIL:	I don't. (BEAT) Do I?
JAI :	If you want to ask her out, ask her out.
NIKHIL:	I'm going to. I've been playing it cool, that's all.
JAI :	Course you have.

JAI IS AMUSED.

CUT TO:

The shape of the scene

I talked about scenes being like mini dramas in their own right and this one could be called Brothers and Sisters. We start with the sisters on their break, in their workplace. (You'll recall from my breakdown that I was worried about the lack of available factory workers, which is why they are in the locker room). Their bosses come in and the two girls go back to work. Simple enough, but it reflects a real workplace situation. It feels like a scene of two halves, however, with the two sisters followed by the two brothers. If I were being critical, I maybe should have crossed the two strands more, played more of the scene with all four of the characters involved. But the scene does have a shape and a dynamic.

What do we learn?

We find out how Gennie is adjusting to being back at work, following her split from Jamie.

We find out that Chas continues to worry about her partner's attitude to her son, which is putting their relationship under pressure.

The sisters are at one in disapproving of their father's attitude to Aaron.

We learn that Maisie is obviously still interested in Nikhil.

We learn that Nikhil, for some reason, and despite his words of denial, is not responding.

We are left wondering why Nikhil is being so slow on the uptake.

So, two plots are progressed:

1. The fallout from Aaron coming out and especially its impact on Chas and Carl.
2. The continuing mystery of Nikhil's recalcitrance.

But, almost as important, we have the fun and the texture of sister and brothers supporting each other, teasing each other and behaving in a way that the audience will recognise and enjoy.

How to play a scene in the pub

I've mentioned several times the importance of communal sets, especially the legendary boozers, as the great British Public House is often called. The factory scene we've just considered involves four characters, but is relatively simple structurally. On the other hand, crossing several story strands involving ten or eleven characters can seem quite daunting. Here is an example, involving eleven characters and several story strands, set in *The Woolpack*, the pub in *Emmerdale*.

Margin Note
Again we have set the script across the page but remember, in a real script it is only on the right hand side.

STUDIO   GENNIE/ LEYLA/ KATIE/ BRENDA/
MAISIE/ CHAS/ MARLON/ RHONA/ PADDY/ JAI/
NIKHIL/ Extras
SC 11 INT THE WOOLPACK BAR 13:02 DAY

LEYLA, KATIE, GENNIE AND CHAS ARE NOW AT A TABLE. GENNIE IS STARTING TO CHEER UP.

LEYLA: So what's this surprise you were on about?

CHAS	:	Nikhil fancies Maisie. Jai was telling him to go for it, weren't he?
GENNIE	:	I'm not sure he's her type.
LEYLA	:	He can't be worse than the dead beats she's been out with before.
CHAS	:	Do you mind? You're talking about my brother.
KATIE	:	And my ex …
LEYLA	:	Yeah, and …

CHAS AND KATIE EXCHANGE A LOOK.

CHAS	:	Fair enough …
LEYLA	:	I reckon he's pretty fit. (TO KATIE) If Maisie doesn't want him she might pass him on to you.
KATIE	:	What is this? Make Katie stick her head in an oven day …
CHAS	:	No, that's Gennie.
GENNIE	:	Shut up.
CHAS	:	Hey …

CHAS INDICATES THE DOOR, WHERE JAI AND NIKHIL WALK IN AND GO TO THE BAR.

MAISIE	:	What can I get you?
JAI	:	Usual?
NIKHIL	:	Great …

AS SHE TURNS TO GET TWO BOTTLES OF BEER, MAISIE NOTICES CHAS, LEYLA, KATIE AND GENNIE LOOKING EXPECTANTLY AT HER.

| MAISIE | : | (SILENT) What? |

MARLON GOES TO RHONA AND PADDY, WITH THEIR LUNCH. RHONA HAS MORE ON HER PLATE THAN PADDY.

| MARLON: | | Two steak pie and chips. (TO RHONA) That'll keep you going as you tramp across those muddy meadows in your fetching little wellies. |

RHONA	:	That's very thoughtful of you.
PADDY	:	I'm doing the calls this afternoon. Rhona's in surgery …
RHONA	:	Wrestling with slavering hounds itching to bite me. (BEAT) And that's just the farmers …
MARLON:		And who can blame them?
RHONA	:	Saucy …
PADDY	:	What's that?

HE POINTS TO SOMETHING EXTRA ON RHONA'S PLATE.

MARLON:		Ratatouille. I've done it a bit differently. I thought you might like to try it.
RHONA	:	Love to …
PADDY	:	What about me?
MARLON:		Rhona's got a more discerning palate than you.
PADDY	:	And she's got more chips …
RHONA	:	(TO MARLON) Thanks …
MARLON:		Mon plaisir …

MARLON GOES. PADDY EYES RHONA'S PLATE.

RHONA	:	Don't even think about it.

SHE TAPS HIS KNUCKLES WITH HER FORK AS BRENDA WALKS IN. SHE HEADS TOWARDS THE BAR, BUT SPOTTING GENNIE, COMES OVER, LOOKING THUNDEROUS.

BRENDA	:	I'm surprised you dare show your face.
CHAS	:	She didn't want to come. I thought it'd cheer her up.
BRENDA	:	She doesn't deserve cheering up, not after what she's done …
KATIE	:	She's said she's sorry …
BRENDA	:	After what happened yesterday, Viv's decided she wants a divorce.
GENNIE	:	She can't have …

BRENDA:	I've never seen her so angry. And I can't say I blame her …
GENNIE :	Nothing happened yesterday …
LEYLA :	Except Viv slapped Gennie. She'd no right to do that.
BRENDA:	I'm not happy about that. (TO GENNIE) But if you'd kept away from him, she'd have had no reason.
GENNIE :	Bob and me bumped into each other. What was I supposed to do, ignore him?
BRENDA:	Yes, that's exactly what you should do. Cross the street when you see him coming …
GENNIE :	Cathy wanted a hug …
BRENDA:	Stop making excuses.
GENNIE :	It's true; she did.
BRENDA:	If you care about those little ones, you'll stay out of their lives. Thanks to you, their mum and dad are going to split up.
GENNIE :	That's not fair.
BRENDA:	But it's a fact. And you'll have to live with it for the rest of your life.

GENNIE FEELS DESPONDENT.
  CUT TO:

So how does it work?

As you'll see, it's a long scene; with eleven characters (you'll notice too, that extras are mentioned in the strap line). It is the type of scene that helps to give Soaps the feeling of community and of lives interacting and over lapping.

What often defeats new writers is the way we move between the different groups or individuals. So let's look at how it works within this scene. We open with a group of friends chatting over a drink. Their attention is drawn to Jai and Nikhil walking into the pub. Maisie, who is working behind the bar, sees them staring and challenges them.

As we look at Maisie, Marlon, who is the chef, appears from the kitchen, behind Maisie and takes food to Paddy and Rhona. As we finish the exchanges between those three characters, we see Brenda, Gennie's mum arrive and go to the group of friends we were with at the beginning of the scene. The intention was to give the scene a fluidity that enabled the director to move seamlessly and organically from one group of characters to another.

It may not be possible to structure a scene quite so organically. In that case, if you want to move from one group of characters to another, you can use the stage direction WE LOOK AT or WE GO TO. "WE" in this instance is the camera, the viewer, all of us looking at what is happening. So for instance, in the scene we have just looked at, the penultimate stage direction could have read thus:

SHE TAPS HIS KNUCKLES WITH HER FORK. **WE GO TO THE DOOR,** AS BRENDA WALKS IN. SHE HEADS TOWARDS THE BAR, BUT SPOTTING GENNIE, COMES OVER, LOOKING THUNDEROUS.

In fact, it wasn't necessary, as Brenda's arrival is implicit in the original stage direction.

"It's all over. I've met someone else ..."

Relationships are at the heart of Soap. People fall in and out of love, betray each other, split up and come back together again; they even get divorced and re-marry. One of the most memorable of all Soap storylines was when Deidre Barlow cheated on her husband Ken with Ken's sworn enemy, Mike Baldwin. It generated enormous publicity and interest. It was the sort of story that had the audience shouting at the screen "Don't do it!" while secretly praying she would, so they could enjoy the fallout. A Soap writer's dream ...

But when we come to these moments in Soap, when a man discovers his wife has been cheating on him, they can't be dealt with in one scene. There is too much to explore, too many complex emotions in play. I have talked about two-handed scenes earlier and counselled against using them too often, but in situations like Ken and Deirdre, they can be compelling. As a writer, you would probably like to write one long scene and go with the flow. However, unless you are lucky enough to be given a two-handed episode, you will have to cut away to other scenes and other stories. This presents two major problems:

1. The conversation between our two characters feels like it should be told in continuous time, in the same place. The stories around it may spread over a much longer period of time. When structuring your episode, you have to try and bring the other stories into line with your main strand.

2. As a Soap writer you cannot "freeze time". By this, I mean that you can't end one scene between the two warring protagonists, cut away to the pub and come back to the very next sentence in the conversation. In those few minutes you have been away, something has to have moved on. You can achieve this by physically moving one or both of the characters or by playing in your mind, conversation that may have taken place while we were away from them. It is tricky.

If you are presented with a story like this, one which runs through the second half of an episode, say, you should try and break it down into the four or five scenes it requires. It may be that you can build in some movement. Maybe one of the characters leaves and we pick them up a couple of scenes later when they come back, or we pick them up in another location; maybe one of them breaks down in tears and when we come back they are wiping their eyes, having recovered their composure.

Here is an example from the Viv-Bob story we've been looking at. It comes in the second of the two episodes, when Bob pleads with Viv to let him have access to his children. It runs across two scenes. The first scene ends like this:

BOB:　　　　No, I'm not having that. I want to see my children …

HE HEADS FOR THE CAFE. VIV PULLS HIM BACK
AND BARS HIS WAY.

VIV :	You can't …
BOB:	Get out of my way.
VIV :	They're asleep.
BOB:	So, I'll look in on them …
VIV :	What are you going to do, shove me out of the way?
BOB:	If I have to.
VIV :	Fine. I can't stop you. But when we get to court I'll tell them exactly what you did. And how's that going to make you look …

BOB IS DEFLATED AND BACKS DOWN.

BOB:	(PLEADING) I can't believe it's come to this.

ON BOB, DESPONDENT.

CUT TO:

We cut away to another story, involving Aaron and we come
back to Viv and Bob. Their next scene begins as follows:

STUDIO   BOB/VIV
SC 18 INT SHOP 21:30 NIGHT

VIV HAS MOVED TO THE DOOR, TO OPEN IT.

VIV :	Go, will you? I'm not interested in anything you've got to say …
BOB:	You've got a short memory.
VIV :	What exactly does that mean?

BOB CLOSES THE DOOR.

A few minutes have gone by. Bob has bounced back from
his despondency but Viv has moved to the door to show
him out.

It means the story has moved on and is not frozen in
time.

This rule applies across the ad break too. The first scene of part two may involve the same characters as the end of part one, in the same place. But you have to build in a sense of time having moved on.

The only exception is when two episodes are divided by half an hour. The two episodes I have discussed played on the same Thursday, one at 7, the second at 8. In this situation, we are allowed to freeze time and pick up from where we left off half an hour before.

Crash, bang, wallop ...

If you become established on a Soap, you may be lucky enough to be invited to write one of the occasional set-piece episodes. This may involve a fire, a flood, a house collapse, a crash or, memorably, a plane dropping on a village. Soaps play these from time to time for several reasons; they:

- pay off big stories and set new ones in motion
- generate publicity and draw attention to the show
- pull in viewers who might not normally watch.

They are, however, expensive to make and consequently are usually entrusted to experienced writers. The aim is to have movie style production values, which is difficult on the much smaller budgets, but history shows there have been some memorable and spectacular Soap stunts.

Perhaps the most famous example of such an "event" in British Soap was when a plane dropped on the village in *Emmerdale* on December 30th 1993. The stunt took three weeks to film at the cost of one million pounds, an astonishing figure in British Soap. But it was worth every penny. The programme, which had been flagging in the ratings, got a massive audience and the fortunes of the programme revived. It may well have saved the programme.

Similarly the now famous tram crash in *Coronation Street* during Christmas 2010 was brilliantly executed and marked a memorable 50th year anniversary.

We may never see such a spectacular episode again, but you may have to write an episode which may contain significant drama that is led not by dialogue but by action.

This will involve the writer in talking to the director, visiting the location and writing a script which will feel a lot more like a film script. It will, of necessity contain a lot of stage directions and probably not much dialogue. It calls on the writer to write visually for the camera. Such episodes naturally depend heavily on the skill of the director, as well as the special effects and stunt teams. But they have to have something to work with. It is the writer's job to give them the bullets to fire (sometimes literally).

It can also be very exciting. I wrote an episode once which involved a car being driven over a cliff edge and exploding into flames on the beach below. I went along to witness the shoot, off the East Coast of Yorkshire. It gave me a valuable insight into the mechanics of filming such an action packed sequence and that, in turn, taught me a lot as a writer.

No dialogue

It isn't only big spectacular episodes that depend on script which use action rather than dialogue. These moments will arise in every script you write: when it is better to tell the story through actions rather than words.

Let's consider a hypothetical situation, in which a man returns home to discover a note. It may be written as follows:

CRAIG WALKS INTO THE LIVING ROOM. HE LOOKS ROUND, TAKING IN THE MESS, THE DIRTY CUPS, MAGAZINES AND NEWSPAPERS STREWN ABOUT. IT LOOKS AS THOUGH SOMEONE HAS LEFT IN A HURRY. HIS ATTENTION IS DRAWN TO THE MANTEL PIECE. HE SEES A NOTE. HE READS IT. HIS FACE DARKENS WITH CONCERN. TOO LATE, HE HEARS A NOISE BEHIND HIM. HE HALF TURNS INTO A BLOW ON A HEAD, FROM AN

UNSEEN ASSAILANT. HE FALLS TO THE FLOOR,
UNCONSCIOUS.
CUT TO:

A task ... or two

Why not flex your muscles? Look at the different types of scenes I have discussed here: the multi- strand scene in a communal set, the emotionally intense two-hander, the stunt driven set-piece and the lower key action sequence. Again, using the Soap of your choice and the characters you feel familiar with try your hand at all three. They will make different demands on you as a writer but they depend on the different skills you will need in writing for a Soap.

10 Getting inside their heads— writing dialogue

An overview

In this chapter, you will confront the challenge of writing dialogue, some of which will be spoken by well-established characters, many of whom have been on our screens for twenty years or more. You will learn the importance of writing economical, memorable dialogue, which avoids cliché and carries story in a subtle and oblique way.

Losing your voice

As I mentioned earlier, by the time you write your first script for a Soap, the chances are you will have "found your voice" as a writer. In other words, you will have experienced that exciting moment when you realise you have come across the style and the tone which is exclusively yours and sets you apart from the millions of other people who have put pen to paper or finger to keyboard. If you doubt the truth of this, consider the works of Alan Bennett, say, Jimmy McGovern, or John Sullivan, creator of BBC tv's *Only Fools and Horses*. They write with an individual distinctiveness that is unique to them. They have been talented and fortunate enough to build a career based on their vision of the world. If that is all you aspire to and you are not prepared to compromise, then writing Soap isn't for you. But do remember that Paul Abbott, Sally Wainwright, Kay Mellor and many more established TV writers, began by writing Soap. Jimmy McGovern himself was one of the original writers of the ground-breaking Channel 4 Television's *Brookside* and wrote something like 80 episodes.

In order to do that, they may at times have had to make some sort of compromise with their own voice as a writer, and inhabit the minds of characters they didn't invent, and may not have much sympathy for. But the job of the Soap writer is to write for all the characters in the show, so you have to embrace it.

There may be occasions when you have to write episodes telling a story you didn't much like when it was pitched. You can—and should—argue your case at conference, but once the decision has been made, you have to give it 100%. If you felt so strongly that you were unable to compromise, then you'd have to resign.

But let's assume you don't …

A task

To illustrate what I mean about voices, try the following exercise. Let's take a classic Soap situation, in which an established married couple confronts a crisis. One of the partners admits to having been conned out of two thousand pounds in a stupid investment.

Write the scene in three ways: first with characters of your own invention; secondly, using Roy and Hayley Cropper from *Coronation Street*; finally, using John and Moira Barton from *Emmerdale*. You can substitute other established couples if you like, but try and get inside the characters, reflecting the way they speak and the relationship they have with their partner. You should come up with three very different scenes and six very different voices. If you don't, then you have a way to go.

The voice of the show

The three main UK Soap operas, *Coronation Street*, *Eastenders* and *Emmerdale*, all have a strong regional identity. (As of course did *Brookside*, which was based on Merseyside). They all sound different. Not every character in these three shows hails from the regions they reflect, but when writing for *Emmerdale*, you should be aware that it takes place in a village in the Dales, *Coronation Street* in the streets of Manchester, while *Eastenders* speaks for itself. In order to write successfully for any of these programmes, your dialogue should seek to capture the flavour and distinctiveness of their inhabitants.

Having said that, we live in an age of social mobility and not everyone in *Emmerdale* will speak with a Yorkshire accent and the East End of London contains people who hail from North of Watford. You have to be prepared to do the lot.

Eh, by gum and other considerations

I am not a huge fan of writing phonetically. In fact, in the two hundred plus scripts I have written for mainstream Soap Operas, I have never done so. When reflecting the flavour of a region, it's more important to capture the rhythm of speech, and to identify words and phrases, which are peculiar to certain areas as well as specific characters.

Have a look at the following extract from an imagined Soapscript, set in Yorkshire, on a Sunday. Bill is a farmer, Jeff his son and Margaret his wife:

BILL	:	You can take that bucket of slop and feed the pigs. And when you've done, we'll go to the pub and you can buy us a pint.
JEFF	:	I were going to take the kids to the swings.
MARGARET:		You do right, love. (TO BILL) And you should go with him. A bit of exercise wouldn't do you any harm.
BILL	:	Give over, woman. I'm having a day of rest.
MARGARET:		Tell me summat I don't know.

Written phonetically, the extract might read as follows:

BILL	:	You can tek that bucket o' slop an' feed t' pigs. And when you've done, we'll go to t' pub and you can buy us a pint.
JEFF	:	I were gonna tekt' kids to t' swings.

97

MARGARET:	You do right, love. (TO BILL) And you should go with 'im. A bit of exercise wouldn't do you any 'arm.
BILL :	Give over, woman. I'm 'avin' a day o' rest.
MARGARET:	Tell me summat I don't know.

The second version is how the actors will probably say the lines. The content is true to their individual characters, the rhythm of the dialogue is true to Yorkshire folk, and they don't need the writer to tell them to drop an aitch or say "tek" instead of "take".

On the other hand, I have left in both versions some usages which may be grammatically incorrect, but reflect the programme.

So Bill says in speech one, "when you've done" instead of "when you've finished". He tells Jeff to buy "us" a pint, not "me", while "Give over, woman", is exactly how he would address Margaret in this scene.

Similarly, Jeff says "I *were* going to take the kids to the swings", instead of *was* and Lisa uses "summat" instead of "something." Although this is not the Queen's English, it is regular usage and, most important, appropriate to the characters who are speaking.

I can't move on without mentioning Seth Armstrong, a wonderful *Emmerdale* character, played for many years by the late and much-missed Stan Richards. Seth was a dyed in the wool Dalesman, who combined poaching with game keeping. And Stan gave him a richness of language that was totally authentic. Thus, he would say "thee" and "thy" instead of you and yours and make his dialogue unique. Sadly, that voice died with Stan, as I fear it may be disappearing in the Dales, but he left us much to cherish.

What is dialogue for?

In his book, *Writing TV Scripts*, (Aber Publishing) Steve Wetton identifies the following five functions of dialogue:

1. Push the Story Along.
2. Give necessary information.

3. Delineate character.
4. Have a subtext.
5. Set up or pay off a funny line.

I have no wish to improve on that list and if you look at the following scene you will see the truth of Steve's list.

SC 9 INT THE WOOLPACK BAR 12:47 DAY

LEYLA AND KATIE ARE AT THE BAR, BEING SERVED BY MAISIE, WHO HANDS OVER TWO ORANGE JUICES, WHEN CHAS AND GENNIE COME IN, GENNIE LOOKING ROUND ANXIOUSLY.

MAISIE :	(TO KATIE) Two pounds forty please.
CHAS :	I wouldn't mind one of them. (BEAT) Gennie …

GENNIE IS LOOKING ROUND.

CHAS :	Will you stop being so twitchy? Katie's offering to buy you a drink.
GENNIE:	Coke, please …
KATIE :	What did you think I am?
CHAS :	A successful local businesswoman with nowt better to spend her money on.
KATIE :	Thanks for reminding me.
LEYLA :	She did say you were successful.
KATIE :	How come, no one's told me?
CHAS :	(TO MAISIE) Hey, and you might want to pour yourself something bubbly. You're in for a treat this dinner time.
MAISIE :	What do you mean?
CHAS :	I can't tell you. That'd spoilt the surprise.
MAISIE :	That's not fair.
CHAS :	You'll find out soon enough.

GENNIE STARTS AS THE DOOR OPENS. A WOMAN WALKS IN. SHE IS RELIEVED IT ISN'T VIV.

GENNIE:	I think I'd better go.
LEYLA :	You've only just got here.
GENNIE:	I know, but …

GENNIE LOOKS SHEEPISH.

CHAS	:	You might as well tell 'em, you told me.
GENNIE:		I'm trying to avoid Viv.
LEYLA	:	So, what's new?
GENNIE:		I've done nothing wrong, well, not this time anyway. I mean she hugged me. Cathy, not Viv. And she had a right go at Bob. Viv, not Cathy … and that's it really …
MAISIE	:	Did anyone understand any of that?

LEYLA AND KATIE SHAKE THEIR HEADS.

GENNIE:		I got up this morning and felt like packing a bag and getting on a bus and never coming back.
LEYLA	:	It's not a bad idea, that. (TO KATIE) What do you reckon?
KATIE	:	I've always wanted to go to the Cotswolds. I like the sound of the name.
MAISIE	:	I wouldn't bother. It's full of toffs in tweed.
LEYLA	:	Rich?
MAISIE	:	And thick, mostly.
CHAS	:	(TO GENNIE) Sounds right up your street …

IN SPITE OF HERSELF, GENNIE SMILES.
   CUT TO:

1.   The scene is part of an ongoing story about Gennie's anxiety about confronting Viv. She once slept with Viv's husband, Bob, while Viv was in prison. They both believed that Viv and Bob's marriage was over but Viv, who has now found out the truth, doesn't see it like that. Two other stories are alluded to: Chas hints to the barmaid Maisie that she is in for a surprise.
2.   We learn that Gennie has had an unfortunate encounter with Viv, which has fuelled her anxiety.
3.   The scene is full of characterful dialogue. This is, first and foremost, a group of female friends. They tease

each other and, in a jokey way, look out for each other. It reads like a group of friends out for a drink, rather than a list of story and character points. They come out organically as the dialogue develops.

4. Several things emerge in the sub text. By pointing out that Katie is a successful local businesswoman, Chas is in fact reminding her that she has recently split from her boyfriend; by commenting on the men in the Cotswolds, Maisie establishes herself as the poshest woman in the group. She's probably the only one who has ever been to the Cotswolds; we also see Chas driving the scene, refusing to let her younger sister, Gennie, get downhearted, teasing her friend Katie and winding up Maisie. It reinforces the pattern of relationships within the group.

5. The tone of the scene is essentially light-hearted banter. Some of the subject matter is serious, but the friends joke about it and the pay off line makes Gennie smile, ending the scene on an upbeat and moving Gennie along from where she was at the start.

Not every passage of dialogue will do all the things in Steve's list, but they will usually do more than one, expressing thoughts and feeling in the sub text and the stage directions.

It is vital that the scene reads, first, like a credible meeting of friends. Get that right and the content takes care of itself.

Writing for household names

While each of the programmes we are discussing has a predominant voice and one which you will need to master, they are also filled with distinctive individuals. You need to put words into the mouths of those people, which are true to them, possibly unique.

I've often been asked how I write for Eddie Grundy, say, or Zak Dingle. It would be glib to say, I don't know, but I can and that's why I got the job. I think this is where the popular misconception that specific writers write for specific characters comes from. In the USA popular series are written in teams, where one may be good at one-liners, another at strong end lines to scenes, but not in the UK.

As a writer, you need an "ear". You need to listen to people you meet, or see on TV and absorb the characteristics of their speech, their rhythms, any little verbal characteristics they might have. Part of this is instinctive, but you can help yourself.

A task

Write down a list of five people. They can be real people, either in the public eye or known to you, or characters from TV or Film. Think about the way they speak. Jot down their individual characteristics. Write dialogue for them.

In order to write for characters like Eddie and Zak, you need to understand who they are and how they relate to other people in their world. You also need a sense of the history of the programme. Once you are part of the writing team, you have access to a researcher and an archivist, to fill in the gaps in your knowledge, but initially, you won't have the benefit of those resources. It goes without saying that you should do your best to get up to speed with the characters, which currently inhabit the show. The more you know about their past, the better. If you are invited to write a trial script, you may be sent past scripts and episodes to watch, as well as a "bible" or book of the show. In the meantime, watch, listen and learn.

If you are lucky enough to write for a Soap, you will find that actors become very protective of "their" characters. They have in many cases been around for a long time and have helped shape the character. When they get a new script to read and learn, they will sometimes question if they feel their character would not express a certain sentiment, or phrase a comment in a certain way. This can be picked up at the Editing stage, by the Producer or Script Editor but if not, they may raise it either before, or sometimes during recording. This can mean a phone call from a Script Editor asking the writer to have another look at the particular dialogue.

Audiences, too, are quick to notice if they feel "so and so would never have done or said that". They rightly feel a certain ownership of the characters and want to see their integrity respected.

You also need to bear in mind characters' relationships with other characters in the show: they may have a long running feud; they may once have been in a relationship together. They may flat out hate one another. All these factors will influence the words you put in their mouths.

When you come to write dialogue for any character, you have to climb inside their head, speak as they would speak, with the feelings and thoughts they would have and in the language they would use. After a while this becomes instinctive, at first it may require an effort.

Writing for new characters

New characters offer a different kind of challenge in terms of dialogue. Before a character arrives in the show, s/he will have been discussed at conference. They are often, but not always, brought in with some kind of link to existing characters or families. I'll be saying more about this later, but for now I want to consider how you find a voice for that character.

The new character will have been given dialogue before they are given their first script. Let's say a new thirty something female character is going to be introduced. She is the sister of one of the existing characters. A brief biography will have been written by one of the writers and the casting director will suggest a short list of actresses to the Producer. Several will be seen and they will be asked to play an *AUDITION* scene, usually with one of the established characters. One of the writing team will write that scene, giving the bulk of the dialogue to the new character. Three or four will be recalled and screen tested, with a new scene and the casting decision will then be made.

The audition scene will often be shown to the writing team at conference, so they can get a feel for the character before they appear in storylines. When the character does appear, several writers will be writing for him/her at the same time. Occasionally, the writers will collectively nail the voice straight away. More likely, one or two writers will find the voice that fits that character. The relevant scenes will be shown to the other writers on the team, so a consistency can be achieved.

Introducing new characters is dealt with in another part of this book, but if you start writing for a Soap Opera, then sooner or later you will get the chance either to introduce a character of your own creation or to write the first scenes of someone new to the show.

This is a tremendous opportunity to define someone who might become a fixture in the programme. And the best way to do that is to establish the way they speak. This is much closer to your own, original writing, when you begin with a blank canvas. And if you can hit upon a distinctive, appealing voice for that character, your stock will rise at the same time as you put your mark on the show.

We're none of us the same — verbal characteristics

Characters both express themselves and define themselves through what they say. In some instances, this may be reflected in a specific verbal mannerism. Fred Elliott, the legendary butcher of *Weatherfield*, comes to mind. He had the habit of repeating certain phrases, with the addition of "I say."

Now, I don't know if this came from the actor, John Savident, or from one of the scriptwriters, but it was a gift to the writing team on *Coronation Street*. It gave clear definition to Fred's speech and had tremendous comic potential. The only pitfall, I suppose, was the temptation to turn Fred into a two-dimensional comic turn, but the writers made sure that never happened, by giving him a son in the form of Ashley and allowing him to play scenes of emotional depth.

Not many characters in Soap have a Fred Elliot style catchphrase but can become recognisable, unique individuals through other means: Roy Cropper in the same show has a tendency to home-spun philosophy, expressed in a slightly formal, archaic and wordy manner. Eric Pollard, in *Emmerdale*, has a jaundiced, cynical world view Sam Dingle, we know, is a simple soul, but that didn't stop him featuring in the moving story around the death of his beloved wife, Alice. Kat Slater, Ena Sharples, Seth Armstrong, Den and Angie, Kim Tate, are or were all iconic characters, each with a clearly defined voice.

In a sense great Soap characters almost write themselves. They are on our screens four or five nights a week, we get to know them as well as our neighbours, and we know them because of what they say.

Before you embark on a career as a Soap writer, you should be confident that you can capture the distinctive speech patterns and attitudes of key characters. You can be certain that it is one of the main things that a producer will be looking for when deciding whether or not to offer you a job.

A task

Try writing short scenes, or monologues for some of the big Soap characters. Read them aloud, test them against the voices you hear on screen and see how close you get.

Keep it off the nose

A common note given by Script Editors to writers is that dialogue is "on the nose". What they mean is that the story point or character point, being expressed in a piece of dialogue, is all on the surface. There is no sub text, nothing for the actor to work with or for the audience to enjoy decoding.

Let's take an imaginary situation in which a wealthy and ruthless landlord, Maurice, is talking to one of his tenant farmers, Arthur, about a proposed rent increase. Here is the "on the nose" version.

ARTHUR: You can't put the rent up without warning. I'm not going to pay.

| MAURICE: | If you don't, I'll send some of my men round to burn down your barn and destroy your tractors. And if that doesn't work, I'll terrorise your wife and kids and seriously damage your health. |

It's extreme, but you'll see that the entire story is given away in one indigestible gobbet of dialogue. Compare it with the following:

| ARTHUR : | You can't do that. I'm not going to pay. |
| MAURICE: | I would, if I were you. |

MAURICE SMILES, MENACINGLY.

What we get from the latter, is, first, a reminder that TV is a visual medium. Much of the impact of Maurice's speech comes from his smile, expressed through a stage direction. More important, however, is **what is left unsaid**. He may indeed end up doing all the things he threatens in version one, but how much more effective and dramatic, to leave Arthur and the audience, guessing.

Bury it

Just as story points can be buried inside a scene, so the intention of dialogue can be hidden. We don't all come out and say what we think, or feel. Whether through shyness or nervousness we hide what we mean behind a smokescreen and arrive at the meaning by an indirect route. Part of your armoury as a writer of Soap dialogue, should be the ability to write subtle dialogue, in which meaning is concealed.

Here is an imagined scene, in which Susan has gained the respect of her three half-brothers, Mark, Nigel and Tony, by outwitting their mutual nemesis, Laura. They sit down to dinner, with Susan's daughter, Lucy.

SUSAN FINISHES FILLING UP THE PLATES. MARK POURS WINE.

| LUCY : | It's dead posh, is this … |
| MARK: | (TO SUSAN) Is she allowed any? (THE WINE) |

LUCY :	Please, mum.
SUSAN:	Go on then. Not too much …

MARK OBLIGES AS NIGEL TURNS TO SUSAN.

NIGEL :	You realise, now you're part of the family, you'll have to take up golf.
SUSAN:	You'll be lucky …
NIGEL :	Good job dad's not alive to hear you say that.
TONY :	You don't have to be any good.
MARK :	Best not to be: winner has to buy the drinks.
LUCY :	That'll never be mum. She's rubbish at games.
SUSAN:	Monopoly's about my limit.
LUCY :	And she cheats at that.
SUSAN:	I do not.
NIGEL :	Doesn't bother us.
LUCY :	It's wrong.
MARK :	We all have to bend the rules, once in a while.

AND HE SMILES AT SUSAN, WITH RESPECT.

On the surface, it's a family meal, but the story point, is the acceptance by the brothers, of Susan as part of the family. So there is the blokeish reference to golf, which leads to the mention of Monopoly and Susan's alleged cheating. And this is what makes the point. Susan got the better of Laura by playing dirty, and this is what has gained the brothers' respect.

The scene could have been written in a much more obvious way:

MARK :	I really like the way you got rid of Laura.
NIGEL :	Me. Too. Very impressive.
SUSAN:	She got what she deserved.
TONY :	I couldn't have put it better myself.
MARK :	Welcome to the family.

And so on …

I suppose there is nothing actually wrong in writing the scene that way, but all it does is advance story, in the most obvious way. There is no texture, and we don't get Lucy's excitement at being part of this new family, nor her insight into her mother's underhand methods. At the same time, we miss out on the reference to the boys' late father, and the golf reference which highlights the blokey world Susan is about to enter.

Break it up

When writing dialogue, avoid the temptation to write in perfectly formed sentences. Your computer will highlight those occasions when you're grammatically accurate. Be prepared to ignore it. In real life, we seldom speak in perfectly formed sentences. (If a character is going to speak formally and correctly, that becomes a character point. Think of Alan Turner in *Emmerdale* or Roy Cropper in *Coronation Street*.)

And if we're under duress or having a laugh and a joke with friends, our mood will be reflected in the way we speak.

Let me give an example of what I mean, again from an imagined drama:

DAVID OPENS THE DOOR TO JUDY. HE IS TAKEN ABACK, AS SHE LOOKS PALE AND DRAWN, HER HANDS TREMBLING SLIGHTLY.

DAVID: Jude, what's the matter? You look terrible …

JUDY IS UNABLE TO SPEAK.

DAVID: Come on, sit down. I'll get you a drink … brandy?

JUDY : Water …

DAVID GOES TO GET JUDY A DRINK OF WATER, AS SHE SITS DOWN.

DAVID: I wondered why you were late. I thought maybe you weren't coming …

JUDY :	It was awful …
DAVID:	What was?

HE HANDS HER A GLASS OF WATER.

DAVID:	You can tell me.
JUDY :	It's Mike …
DAVID:	What's he done now?
JUDY :	The usual … drinking … I thought he was going to … (KILL ME) …
DAVID:	(REASSURING) It's okay ….
JUDY :	It was stupid. A dress … new … he accused me. (BEAT) … he accused me of having … (AN AFFAIR) I didn't mean to … I was frightened. He frightened me.
DAVID:	What did you do?
JUDY :	The things he said. He was screaming at me. (BEAT) I didn't mean to do it. But I think I've … (KILLED HIM).

SHE BEGINS TO SOB, UNCONTROLLABLY.

All good, heightened, melodramatic stuff! You'll notice several things about the way the scene is written. Judy's words are disjointed, her thoughts are incomplete, and the sequence of events is not described in neat, chronological order.

The device of using … three dots is employed. This is a good way of showing incomplete thoughts, or of a sentence tailing off. It shouldn't be overused, but is very useful in certain circumstances.

On several occasions, the completion of a sentence or a thought is indicated in brackets using upper case letters e.g., (KILL ME) or (AN AFFAIR). This is to let the actor know what she is trying to say. The audience is left to fill in the blanks.

Stage directions are also used. Thus we see Judy shaking slightly, unable to speak and at the end, dissolving into tears. Remember what I have said before, you are writing in a visual medium and you don't simply use dialogue to tell your story.

I have also used one Stage Direction to indicate the precise tone and meaning of a line of dialogue, when David says: (REASSURING) It's okay …

I am not a great advocate of this type of stage direction. Some writers use them much more frequently. I was once asked to look at the script for a Radio Play by a new writer, which read something like this. (This version is completely made up).

JOHN:	(ENQUIRING) The nine forty five?
MARY:	(TETCHY) That's what he said …
JOHN:	(DEFENSIVE) Okay …
MARY:	(ANGRY) Why does he never do what I ask him?
JOHN:	(CONCILIATORY) It could have been a misunderstanding …
MARY:	(SUDDENLY VULNERABLE) He doesn't love me any more …

And on and on it went, page after page, every line of dialogue prefaced by an emotionally specific stage direction. There are several reasons why I think this is a bad idea.

It makes the script "read" badly. Reading it for the first time, the constant presence of such directions would interrupt the flow of the dialogue and it would seem stilted.

Secondly, by and large, actors don't like them. They can feel offended, that they're not being credited with the skill and intelligence to interpret the meaning of the line. As a writer, you should feel confident that the meaning and emphasis is clear from the skill with which you have written the dialogue. Equally, you should be open to the possibility that the actor and/or director will see the line in a different, **but better**, way than you intended.

I once worked with a director who expunged every single stage direction from the script before the actors saw them. This included apparently essential directions like, for instance, JOHN BREAKS INTO A RUN or DAVID GRABS JULIE'S PURSE, which had nothing to do with emotional content. The director wanted the freedom to choreograph and interpret the scene in entirely her own way. That was taking it a bit far and was very frustrating for the writer ...

There have been occasions when a script editor has asked me to include specific stage directions, where an actor might be a little slow on the uptake. In this respect (IRONY) is useful. A line intended to be ironic but delivered straight, can destroy the entire meaning of a scene.

Don't play ping pong

Dialogue can be written in a very predictable way, with characters appearing to know what's coming next and with no element of surprise, and no characters saying something that comes out of left field. This can also be reflected in characters speaking in single sentences of similar length, resulting in a predictable rhythm. For instance:

MARTIN:	I walked down the hill at five o'clock.
GEORGE:	I suppose it was busy.
MARTIN:	People coming home from work, you know.
GEORGE:	I got stuck in a traffic jam on the bypass.
MARTIN:	That's why I prefer to walk.
GEORGE:	Since your heart attack.
MARTIN:	The doc says I need the exercise.

The dialogue plods along, one thought leading to another, the characters telling one another things they already know. It is, quite simply, dull.

It could read as follows:

MARTIN:	I walked home.
GEORGE:	You want to be careful, with your ticker.
MARTIN:	Doc says it's good for me, as long as I take it easy. Stop me having another heart attack.
GEORGE:	Wish I'd joined you. Traffic was murder ...

We get the same information, but in a less predictable and more characterful way. It feels more like an actual conversation and less like a list.

Question and answer

Equally predictable can be scenes in which one character asks questions throughout and the other answers them. This can apply to apparently obvious scenes, like a police officer interviewing a suspect. For example:

DC SMITH: What time did you leave the club?
MICKY   :   Two o'clock.
DC SMITH: Did anybody see you leave?
MICKY   :   No.
DC SMITH: And where did you go then?
MICKY   :   Home?
DC SMITH: And was anybody in when you got there?
MICKY   :   They were all in bed.

All perfectly fine, up to a point, but consider how it could have read:

DC SMITH: What time did you leave the club?
MICKY   :   Two o'clock, I told you.
DC SMITH: And let me guess, nobody saw you …
MICKY   :   I doubt it. It was dark.
DC SMITH: You can leave the jokes to me.
MICKY   :   You're doing me head in.
DC SMITH: That's the idea. (BEAT) And I suppose the luscious Sandy was waiting for you when you got home.
MICKY   :   Leave her out of this.

It's not perfect, but it has conflict, it suggests the characters of the two men and hints at a history between them. It goes beyond the plodding ritual of question and answer. We get the same information but in a livelier and more original way.

We need to talk and I'll be there for you twenty four seven

I know clichés are part of everyday speech and we all use them, but it's the job of a writer to write in an original way and to put memorable words into the mouths of characters, not trot out the most obvious phrase that comes to mind. You should aim to be fresh and inventive, not stale. When writing dialogue, if the first phrase that comes to mind is a cliché, think again. Remember, your job is to get inside the heads of your characters and find innovative and distinctive ways of speaking.

Some clichés have been around for years and become part of the language: phrases like "fresh as a daisy", "cool as a cucumber" and "tough as old boots". The list is a long one but I don't think there's any excuse for using one of these old chestnuts (and there's another one …)

Each of those examples could be replaced by a more inventive and original phrase. It will be harder work to come up with something new but how much more satisfying to coin a memorable piece of dialogue that is all your own. A producer will read a phrase like "she's no spring chicken" and at best pay it no heed, at worst gain a negative impression of you, but if you express the same thought in a new way, it will help your script to leap off the page.

Another type of cliché is the buzz word or phrase, which comes into vogue and finds its way into our everyday language, through the media or through, literally, word of mouth. I suppose "I'll be there for you" falls into this category. It is of course the theme song from *Friends* and maybe that's where it comes from. We all know what it means, but over use has moved it dangerously close to the land of cliché. There are other ways of expressing that sentiment. In Soap, as in all drama, characters will at times want to express their support for someone they love and care for. I try and find something that doesn't rely on that over used phrase.

It is of course possible to make a character point about someone who speaks through clichés, whether they be old or new, but my feeling is, they would lack the necessary variety and texture of speech to stay the course. (It is more likely to be an asset in sitcom, say, where the aim is to make the audience laugh and where characterisation may be established in broader brush strokes).

I could reserve a special category for the phrase, "we need to talk", which springs up like a particularly virulent weed throughout television drama, including Soap. It is often used as the "tag" line of a scene, before we cut away to return a couple of scenes later to hear what the characters need to talk about. Again, I think it is unnecessary. I'd rather come in hard on the conversation itself, or through the kind of oblique dialogue we've been looking at earlier. This will keep the pace of the script tighter and more economical. Chiefly, though, I object to it because it has become a cliché and thus it sounds tired and dull.

If you're in any doubt about this, try and recall moments which have stood out for you in film or TV drama over the years. I suggest that they are as likely to be pieces of dialogue, as bits of action.

Remember Oz in *Auf Wiedersehen Pet*, sharing his sexual adventure and telling Dennis that sex is in its infancy in Gateshead, or Yosser Hughes in the confessional in *Boys From the Blackstuff* telling the priest, Dan, in the confessional, that he was desperate.

Some characters lend themselves to quirky and inventive dialogue more easily than others, a Bob Hope, say or a Norris Cole, but even when writing for characters who speak more naturalistically, try and find an original way of putting words in their mouth.

If you're still not convinced, let me share with you a line from my first rejection letter many years ago. (I was very young but I reckon I deserved it.) "If you're going to put words in someone's mouth, they've got to be worth saying."

For ****'s sake don't bother

The rule about swearing and Soap, is, quite simply, don't. Mainstream Soap Operas are broadcast in the pre-watershed period before 9 o'clock. There are strict rules of compliance, governing what can and can't be allowed by way of dialogue and action. And swearing is very definitely a non-starter. TV drama is governed by Compliance, which determines what can be portrayed and spoken at what time. All the popular Soaps go out before the watershed time of nine o'clock and this limits what we can show on screen and the language we can use. At *Emmerdale* we are given a list which tells us how far we can go in terms of language, and which words we can and can't use.

In spite of that, Soaps have over the years, dealt with tough, adult themes in convincing ways. And if we can't show graphic scenes of sex and violence then does it really matter? After all, sometimes the imagination is more powerful than explicit images.

I have often heard it said such and such a character would swear like a trooper in real life. Well, maybe they would, but not at 7-15 on a Wednesday night in front of a family audience of millions. And the argument that the kids of today have heard it all before won't wash, either. So, rather than rail against a perceived restriction to your art, embrace it as a challenge. In drama, as in life, swearing can be a lazy excuse in terms of language. Try and find new ways to express anger, frustration, or whatever it is that might impel one to swear. It will help you to find that originality which makes you stand out of the crowd.

Finding your voice all over again

A number of my friends and family members, who watch *Emmerdale*, claim they can tell an episode I have written without seeing my name on the credits. I used to be sceptical about this, but I think I can do the same with my fellow writers, as well as certain, distinctive writers on *Coronation Street* and other shows.

And this, I would argue, is when you arrive as Soap writer: the point at which your voice manages to be heard through the collective endeavour that is a continuing drama series. It IS possible and it gives you the joy of individual creativity within the potentially constricting framework of Soap. And at the heart of that individuality, is dialogue, the words you put in the mouths of those well-loved characters.

What you shouldn't do, however, is use established characters as a mouthpiece for your own beliefs and preoccupations (unless they are shared by that particular character). This doesn't happen often, partly because actors are very protective of "their" characters and will question whether or not they would say it. But sometimes things get through the editing and recording process.

You are not the character

If you want to express your own deeply felt opinions and beliefs, then Soap is not the most obvious place to do it. You'd be better off writing a play for Radio or Theatre. Certain characters may share some of your principles but even so you have to write those characters in their own voice, not your own.

A writer with whom I once worked held strong feminist principles. She would, sometimes, properly, argue from that standpoint when trying to pitch or influence the direction of stories. That was her prerogative and her principles were sincerely felt. However, on more than one occasion, she put feminist propaganda into the mouths of characters who did not share those views, and it jarred.

On another occasion, a different writer had a seventy year-old, rather old-fashioned character talk about House Music, not as something which puzzled her, but as if she knew what it was about.

It is understandable to want to put across one's own beliefs and idiosyncrasies, but putting inappropriate words in the mouths of characters is not the way. Both those examples should maybe have been picked up in edits, but they got through. Many of the audience may not have noticed, but viewers, like actors, jealously guard the integrity of the characters they love and one has to respect that.

But there are ways of letting your own voice come through and with practice and experience you can find them. It makes the job even more rewarding.

Writing sharp, witty, dramatic, original dialogue should be your goal. It is one sure way to make you stand

out from the crowd and to enable you to remain valuable to a team of writers. Work on it, hone it, reject the obvious and look for the new, fresh way of expressing it.

A task

Write a scene for four characters, either using existing Soap characters, or ones of your own devising. Two of them have fallen out over something, the third knows and tries to make peace, and the fourth is in a state of ignorance as to what is going on.

They don't all have to be in the scene at the beginning.

Write the scene in two different ways: as a light-hearted comic scene and as a more serious dramatic one. Make sure you have a hold on the different characters and a clear sense of how they speak. Give them distinctive voices.

11 My Elsie Tanner of long ago ... characters in Soap ...

An overview

This chapter will look at what makes a successful Soap character. It will show how some develop into iconic figures and how others fall by the wayside. It will give an insight into how the character mix in the various Soaps is created and how that mix will change, over time.

Icons

In the fifty years of TV Soap operas, certain characters stand out. They have entered the popular imagination and are cherished by the viewers, who come to regard them as people they know. Even the out and out villains hold a special place in their hearts. You could make your own list, but for starters, how about Ena Sharples and Elsie Tanner, Den and Angie, Kim Tate and Annie Sugden.

Ena was the tough, judgemental, overbearing woman, who was typical of so many of her generation. They had lived through the years of Depression and War, experienced privation and loss, were bolstered by their strict Methodist faith and had little truck with the new, more carefree attitudes of the nineteen sixties. My maternal grandmother was a bit like Ena, not so fierce, but forged by the same kind of tough life in a Northern city. But then I suppose she was like a lot of people's Grandmas, which was why she was so successful.

Elsie Tanner was iconic for very different reasons. The polar opposite to Ena in her morality and approach to life, Elsie lived life to the full and had a chaotic history of heartbreak with men. The audience, I'm sure wished she would one day find happiness, knowing that she never would. Her onscreen clashes with disapproving Ena were the stuff of legend.

Den and Angie were the classic "can't live with you can't without you" couple, whose battles in the *Queen Vic* were compulsory viewing for millions of fans. Hard to believe in our multi-channel era, but the Christmas episode in which Den served Angie with her divorce papers was watched by something like 26 million viewers.

Annie Sugden was the matriarch par excellence, ruling *Emmerdale Farm* and its men folk with a firm and steady hand. It was a hard life and Annie was entirely credible and one of the reasons the show became the success it was.

Last but not least, Kim Tate, who began life as Frank Tate's PA at Home Farm, and ended up betraying him, seeing him off and ruling the roost herself for a while. She even managed the Bobby Ewing (*Dallas*) feat of being brought back from the dead.

A task

The characters above all come from the past. Are there any characters currently in Soaps who have that kind of stature? Are there any more from different eras that deserve to be in that list? If so, what makes them iconic? Cain Dingle, Phil Mitchell or Steve Macdonald perhaps …

The mix

All of the characters mentioned above, are played as fully-rounded, three dimensional human beings, by talented and skilful actors. If they weren't so rich and complex, then they wouldn't have lasted so long and achieved the status they had. And that is what those of us writing Soap, want our characters to become: complex, difficult, unpredictable, allowing us to tell complex and unpredictable stories.

Each of the Soaps has to have a mix of characters, to enable it to tell a wide range of stories. Hollyoaks will clearly aim for a younger demographic, but the other three Soaps we have discussed, *Coronation Street, Eastenders,* and *Emmerdale,* will aim for a mix in terms of age, gender, ethnicity and sexuality. Social class is less of an issue. Soaps tend to portray predominantly working class, or lower middle class lives. *Emmerdale*, being rural has a wider social spectrum, and once featured the aristocratic Lady Tara. But more often than not, the occupants of Home Farm are self-made men and women, who have made their own money and their own luck: Frank Tate and Tom King for instance.

If you consider the casts of *Coronation Street*, *Emmerdale* and *Eastenders*, you will find characters right across the age spectrum: from new born babies to elderly and possibly quite frail men and women. The shows seek to represent life as it is, and to aim to a wide audience, so there needs to be something for every age group. The youth market, 18–34, is the one most eagerly pursued by programme makers but that doesn't necessarily mean telling stories featuring that demographic. A good character is a good character, whatever his or her age. A piece of research a few years ago revealed the average age of the *Coronation Street* and *Emmerdale* viewer to be in their mid-fifties, while *Eastenders* had a younger appeal, with the average being in the mid-forties.

Characters come and go and from time to time the programmes will review the mix that they have. They will bear in mind a number of criteria:

They will want to maintain a balanced mix of gender in specific age groups: pre-teens, teenagers, twenty and thirty somethings, characters in their forties and fifties as well as a number of older characters. Occasionally things get out of kilter. In the twenty and thirty bracket, for instance, you will want to tell romantic and relationship based stories, as people fall in and out of love, get married and start families. It's no use, therefore, having six women and one man in, say the 20–30 age bracket. It restricts the stories one can tell.

This isn't to say that stories should be limited to specific age brackets and some will cross age boundaries, but teenagers have to have people of their own age with whom to interact, as well as mums, dads and grandparents to rebel against.

Each Soap will have a number of key families at its core. The pattern of family life has changed dramatically since Soaps began, and the shows will seek to reflect this.

Soaps have long felt able to reflect the lives of gay people, and each has told stories about people "coming out" and coming to terms with their sexuality. The increasing challenge is to tell stories about gay characters that don't simply deal with their sexuality, but with all aspects of their lives.

Emmerdale has introduced a blind character, played by a blind actress and other Soaps are showing a readiness to present characters with disabilities: and if they are played by actors with those disabilities, then so much the better.

This doesn't come out of some slavish pursuit of Political Correctness, but from a genuine wish to portray the lives of all members of our complex and varied society. Hence, too the increasing numbers of members of ethnic minorities in the shows. To represent life in the East End of London or Manchester and not reflect the ethnic mix of those areas would be to distort the reality of life in those places and *Emmerdale*, too, increasingly shows representatives of ethnic groups beyond White Anglo-Saxon as it seeks to reflect the changing patterns of rural life.

To try and cover all those bases in terms of character is an ongoing process. Soaps have limited cast numbers. If there were too many cast members, it would be impossible to give them all sufficient screen time.

So, inevitably, from time to time, things get out of kilter and the balance has to be redressed by new characters arriving as established characters leave.

Plugging the gaps

So how do we bring in a new character?

First of all there is an issue to address: does the new character have any links to an existing character or family, or do we bring in a new character with no links at all?

Attaching a new character to an existing character group is the more secure option. It gives them an established character mix to play against. It helps with casting, as the actors called for audition can be seen with the characters they will be interacting with most often.

Let me give examples of both approaches from *Emmerdale*:

1. In the late 1990's, a new temporary barmaid was introduced to work at *The Woolpack*. The character's name was Bernice Blackstock, a lively, attractive woman in her late twenties. Originally on a short term contract, she made a very strong impression, and the producer and writing team decided to make her a permanent cast member. She was so successful, and popular, that an extended family was built around her. In came her mother, Diane, her estranged sister Nicola, and her father Rodney. Her husband briefly came into the programme but after her divorce, she married the vicar, Ashley and they had a child, Gabrielle, or Gabby. Bernice became involved with her sister Nicola's fiancé, Carlos and ruined their wedding day. She enjoyed a turbulent and dramatic few years in the show, before the actress who played her decided to leave for pastures new.

   But her legacy lives on. Her mother, Diane, is still at the heart of the show. She was married for a time to Jack Sugden, head of the farming family, and became landlady of *The Woolpack*. Her wayward sister Val arrived a few years later and is now involved with another long standing character, Eric Pollard. Ashley remarried but Gabby has been brought up by him, doted on by her grandfather Rodney. Nicola, too, is still in the show, after leaving for a few years, married to a member of another key family, Jimmy King. (And off screen, Bernice too lives on, in Brighton. If we need to lose any of her family when a cast member is on leave, they often head to the South Coast!).

So, from a short term contract, a dynasty has grown, and occupies a place at the heart of the show.

2. On the other hand, the Dingles were brought into *Emmerdale* in the early-90s as a family from hell. Rough, tough and lawless, they comprised Zak, Nellie and three sons, Butch, Ben and Sam. At the time, many viewers were horrified by their antics and appearance. Over the years, many Dingles have come and gone, and from the original group only Zak and Sam remain. They have mellowed with age but remain at the centre of the show and provide it with some its most vivid characters.

Many of them have biblical names: apart from Zak, here have been Shadrach, Cain, Eli, Genesis and Noah, to name but a few, although their behaviour is often far from righteous. Over thirty have passed through the show, some only fleetingly, others becoming Dingles through marriage, and many are writ large in the history of the show: Tina, Mandy and Butch, for example, while of the current generation, Cain, Charity, Marlon and Debbie, to mention but four, remain at the heart of the programme, and have been involved in some of the biggest stories in the history of the show, while remaining hugely popular with the audience, having been voted the most popular family in Soap in a magazine poll.

Family values

As I said earlier, families remain at the heart of the main Soaps, and sometimes they will introduce whole families all in one go. This is not easy. It is difficult enough to introduce one character successfully, but to manage four or five individuals at the same time is very tough indeed. Each member of the family has to become established and to bed into the programme, getting involved in stories and the family group has to have credible relationships, to feel believable. The casting has to be spot on, to ensure a credible and interesting blend. When it works, the effect can be memorable: the arrival of the Slaters in *Eastenders* was spectacular, as was that of the Battersbys in *Coronation Street*. Both families played a big part in their respective shows for many years.

The Kings in *Emmerdale* were introduced differently, one at a time, over a period of weeks, as they undermined and took over an established local business by underhand means. Tom, the father, and three of his sons, Matthew, Carl and Jimmy were introduced. Later on came Max, Sadie, Carrie, Scarlett and Rosemary. Carl, Jimmy and Scarlett remain, although the family lost much of the power and wealth it once had, generating terrific stories along the way.

Sometimes it doesn't work out. The Marsden family entered *Emmerdale* in 2003. A lot of work was done on their back story and their relationships inside and outside the family. But they just didn't work. There was no one single factor to blame. It could have been the chemistry between the family members, the way we writers wrote for them, the stories we gave them to play, or more likely a combination of all three. After about 18 months, they were gone.

Who are they?

Before a new character appears on screen, a lot of work will have been done. Apart from writing the audition scenes, as mentioned before, one of the writers or a member of the story team, will have drawn up a biography, giving details of the character's life history to that point. This will be their **BACK STORY** and may be revealed as the character becomes established in the show. Many characters, as Soap watchers will know, come with dark, murky secrets, waiting to be blown at a suitably dramatic moment. These are usually, but not always, worked out in advance, and a long term story arc plotted before the character arrives on screen. There is nothing worse than a character arriving and drifting. It is puzzling for the audience and potentially demoralising for the actor.

There will also be an outline of the character's defining character traits. This, however, will not be prescriptive. The chosen actor will bring his or her own ideas and strengths to the character, the writers will see this in performance and the character will grow, perhaps in a new and surprising direction. Watching a character evolve and develop over time is one of the most fascinating and exciting aspects of being part of a Soap writing team.

A task

Invent your own Soap family. Write biographies for each of the family members and indicate where they will fit in the programme you choose. What is their history, how do they get on with each other, who do they love and hate? Write them in scenes, on their own, or with existing characters.

Do the same thing for a new member joining an existing family group.

Character types

It seems ironic, when seeking to develop three dimensional characters, to talk in terms of types, but they provide a starting point. I'm sure you'll recognise the following types in all the mainstream Soaps.

The Super bitch
The Love Rat
The tart with the heart
The girl (or boy) next door
The busybody
The gossip
The loser in love
The villain
The sex bomb
The matriarch (or patriarch)

A brief task

If you are a regular viewer of Soap, try and find past or present characters to fit the above definitions. If not, as you begin to watch see if you can recognise these types. Create your own examples of one or more of these types.

You might also add to the list. There are almost certainly some missing.

They may seem like two-dimensional descriptions, but the most memorable examples of these types will be far from two-dimensional. It can be a useful short hand for the producer and writing team when looking to find gaps in the character mix and finding ways to plug them. If, for instance, the show lacks someone who could credibly be called, a "villain" then it is missing out on a wide range of stories that can be generated by such characters. As someone once said, the devil has the best tunes. And villains don't have to be gun toting gangsters. They may not be criminals at all, but express their malevolence through the emotional damage they do to those around them.

Front covers and gongs

Soaps are big business. As I've said before, they generate huge audiences and vast amounts of income. Their stars become national celebrities and find themselves being interviewed on TV and in print, and adorning the front covers of a wide range of magazines, which seek to satisfy the public's interest in these shows. Each programme will have a Press Office, whose job it is to keep their stars in the public eye (for the right reasons!) and to promote the programme as energetically as possible. Some actors are more enthusiastic than others about this degree of exposure but most accept that it is part of the job.

Soaps are now included in the annual BAFTA awards (in the continuing drama category) and feature in several other polls, organised by various magazines. They even have their own specific award ceremony, the annual Soap awards. All the Soaps covet recognition in these various competitions. It generates publicity for the programmes, but more important, rewards and recognises the hard work put in by the vast array of talented people who work on the shows.

Bearing in mind the list of types above, the Soap awards has categories for Best Soap Villain and Best Soap Bitch as well as Best Newcomer, Dramatic Performance (Male and Female) and so on. There is even nod to the writers in Best Single Episode and Best Soap. Some awards are voted for by the general public, others by panels of professionals. But whoever votes for them, if you win, you feel ten feet tall.

Celebrity casting

I mention the awards in order to emphasise once again the context in which Soaps operate. It is Show Biz as well as drama. And if you wish to write for one you have to embrace that reality. From time to time, Soaps will cast big name "stars" from outside the world of drama. It is something of a gamble. Acting in a Soap puts enormous demands on even the most seasoned professional, with the pressures of the schedule and lack of rehearsal time. The benefits in terms of publicity and exposure for the show in casting a "star" are obvious, but if they don't deliver the quality of performance required then no amount of celebrity can protect them. Having said that, failure is rare, and many so called celebrities go on to become permanent fixtures in Soap.

It's worth mentioning that Soaps also increasingly attract actors of the highest calibre, with distinguished performers from the world of stage and screen adding to the high quality of performance on show week in and week out.

Kings of the castle

Certain roles in Soap are vital to the balance and success of the show. Each of them has a power base, a place where some of the key players live and/or work. It is vital to get the character mix right in these places. In *Emmerdale*, for instance, it is Home Farm, in *Coronation Street*, arguably the Underworld factory. What both have in common is that they are owned by people with power and people with control over the lives of others. They can hire and fire and use their influence to impact on others. Both establishments can boast a roll call of some of the most significant players in the history of the shows.

Last orders please

Pubs are at the heart of a Soap and it is important to have the right people running and owning them. As I said earlier, pubs are communal sets where different story strands are played in tandem, but they should also be places where the audience wants to go, to be entertained by the people that run them. In real life, getting the right landlord/landlady and bar staff is vital to the success of the business. The same is true in Soap. They can be front of house one minute, keeping order, doling out advice, breaking up fights and barring an obstreperous drunk. The next minute they'll be behind the scenes, playing out their own dramas.

Think of Peggy Mitchell, Bet and Alec Gilroy, Diane Sugden, big characters all, at the very centre of the worlds we create.

The way out

Characters leave Soaps for a variety of reasons. Sometimes, the actor chooses to leave, in order to develop his or her career, to seek new challenges. They want to play a variety of roles and not be tied down to one. They will sometimes ask if the door may be left open for their return, and this often happens. The writers' task in those circumstances is to create a credible reason for that character to go, without compromising the possibility of their coming back. They will come up with an **OUT STORY**. The nature of the story will depend on the status and significance of the character. Someone with a long and distinguished history on a programme isn't simply going to catch a bus out of town. There will be a definite reason, which will have been established in the weeks and months before they leave, Again, the principle applies, the story should have consequences.

From the actor's point of view, there is a degree of risk in leaving, in the hope of coming back. In their absence, the show will have moved on and other characters may have filled the space they occupied. Or, they may indeed return only to find that they no longer seem to fit and their second stint could be brief. On the other hand, many return and are welcomed with open arms, slotting back seamlessly into the programme.

Sometimes, of course, the actor may not be granted his or her wish to have the door left open. They may find themselves being killed off. Deaths are an inevitable part of all drama but in Soap they should be used sparingly. There is a saying in Soap that you should never "waste" a death. In other words, the terrible event should have an impact on those left behind; it should be someone who has occupied a significant part in the drama and should therefore have consequences.

There are occasions when the actor may leave the show against his or her wishes. This will usually be decided around the time that their contract comes up for renewal. Such decisions are never taken lightly; after all, people's livelihoods are at stake. Sometimes, it involves the departure of a well-established character that may have been in the programme for a long time. They will have proved, over time that they have a valid place in the show, but a point can be reached where there are no more stories left to tell with that character. The choice is either to let them stay, as texture, not really generating story, or to bite the bullet and let them move them on.

Conversely, the character leaving may have been in the show for a short time. It doesn't mean the person playing them is a bad actor, it may be that the character envisaged by the Producer and writers, hasn't really emerged from the performance, or, even if it has, it isn't quite what the show wants or needs. Either way, it is sad to see anyone lose their job. Outside the world of Soap, insecurity is part of an actor's life, as it is a writer's, so I guess we all sign up for it.

You should know now what makes a Soap character work, how a balance is found across the cast of such a programme and the responsibilities the writer has in helping to create and shape those characters.

A Final task

Identify a gap in a Soap, where you feel a new character would fit.

Write a biography of that character, as succinctly as you can, giving his or her dominant character traits.

Say where you think that character would fit into the mix. Where would s/he work, live, who would they interact with?.

Write an audition piece for that character.

Write that character's first scene in the show.

Part II
Staying in

12 You've only just begun

An overview

By now, you have looked at all the component parts that go to make up a Soap script: the layout, the structure, the dialogue, the characters and the kind of stories you can tell. This chapter will explain the day-to-day realities of the Soap writer's working life.

So let us suppose that you have been given the opportunity to write for one of the established Soaps. In some ways, your journey has only just started. You will have a few potentially life changing decisions to make, such as whether or not to give up the security of a job, if you have one. You certainly won't have security as a writer, as you'll only be as good as your last script.

The first TV producer I ever met (I didn't get the job) told me that any writer could write two or three cracking scripts when they started out but the real challenge would some twelve months down the line, when your child was ill, your marriage was breaking up, you were up to your eyes in debt and you had two days to turn a script round. He was exaggerating, of course, but there is an element of truth in what he said. You need to be aware of what the reality of being a writer is like, in order to prepare yourself.

For a start, you'll be the new kid on the block, and as I said before, you'll meet many established writers. Some will be generous with their help and advice, others may not. They won't bother getting to know you and might assume you'll last a few months and then disappear.

As some do ...

So you need to develop a thick skin and you need to have a belief in your own ability and talent, because, it will be challenged and you will feel insecure.

135

Deadlines

You will be expected to deliver scripts on time, to meet deadlines. After a few months, you could have a first, second and third draft on the go at the same time, while being expected to come up with stories for a forthcoming long term conference.

Some writers, like me, make a point of organising their time and like the security of being finished ahead of the deadline. Others need the motivation of being close to a deadline before kicking into gear and burning the midnight oil to get the script written. You may already know what kind of writer you are; if you don't, you'll soon find out.

Emergencies

In the world of TV production, as in all walks of life, you need to expect the unexpected. You may think a script has been safely put to bed, only to get a phone call informing you that an actor has been taken ill and you need to put a different character in a couple of scenes, while still playing the same story beats or a few scenes based round a camping expedition have had to be re-located to an interior set due to snow, or there has been a last minute change of heart about a particular storyline ...

All the above have happened to me and any Soap writer will have similar tale to tell. It is part and parcel of the job. It can be inconvenient; it can ruin your planned night out, or wreck your holiday plans, but ask yourself ... what would you rather be doing with your life? My best advice is to take such slings and arrows in your stride.

13

You won't get it right first time ... or even the second ...

An overview

One of the most difficult adjustments to make when you become a professional writer is to get used to the editing process. Every script you deliver will go through several drafts before it appears on screen. How many drafts, will vary from programme to programme. This chapter will explain how the process works and help prepare you to deal with it.

The editing process

When you have turned your storyline document into an episode, you will deliver it to the Production Centre. It is no doubt stating the obvious, but this will be done via an attachment to an email. You will have had between 2–3 weeks to produce your draft and you may wait a further length of time before you have the edit.

Before anyone speaks to you about your script, it will have been read by a number of people: the script editor who is assigned to that script and possibly some of his or her fellow script editors; the script producer, who has oversight of the entire process; the researcher will also read it, making sure that, for instance any legal content or medical detail is accurate.

Scripts will probably be read in small clusters, usually the Production Block (on *Emmerdale* this is four episodes). A script editor will be assigned to those four, which helps continuity. The series producer may read the first draft, or may wait until the second. It can often depend on the many other pressures on their time.

The people who have read your script will then meet and go through it in detail, sharing their notes and observations.

The script editor responsible for your script will take detailed notes, ready to pass them on to you. They will then fix a mutually agreeable time to go over your script. This could be face- to-face, involving the writer going to the production centre, or it could be done over the telephone. An edit can last between one and four hours, depending on the number and complexity of the notes, the style of the script editor and the willingness of the writer to accept the notes. (More on this later).

The script editor may first give you Headline notes. These are general notes, affecting a particular story running across your episode. There may have been a change of emphasis in the telling of that story across the block, you may not have quite nailed the precise tone or balance the producer is looking for, an extra scene may be required and so on ...

Once the headline notes have been given, the script editor will go through your script page by page and give you detailed notes. These notes fall into a number of categories. In no particular order.

Continuity

For instance, you may be repeating a beat that has already been played in a previous episode. You may have picked up a particular story at the wrong point. Something may have been said and done in a previous episode of which you were unaware.

Most of these changes are not the writer's "fault". Changes will have been made further back in the editing process, which have a knock-effect on your episode.

Getting continuity right is vital to the integrity of long-running series. If it is wrong, the audience will notice. Before a block of scripts are finally published, a senior script editor will read them solely from the point of view of continuity.

Story changes

A story, when told through a script, can look very different to the one that was pitched and agreed at conference and set down in a storyline document. It is the producer's responsibility to make the programme as compelling as possible and if they can see better way of telling the story, they will want to make changes. You may not agree, of course ...

Your writing

These are the notes that some script editors find hardest to give and some writers find hardest to receive. They are basically notes which mean "you could do better". This may be by making a scene more dramatic or funnier, by making a piece of dialogue less clichéd or less on the nose or by building up the impact of your cliff-hanger scene. You may be told that you haven't got the voice of a particular character right.

Writers are different. Some deliver close to the desired script first time. Others need a bit of pushing through several drafts to get it right.

These notes can be confidence-shredding to writers, especially new ones, but you'll have to deal with them. My best advice is to be positive, and to accept the fact that no one can get it right first time (although you may have re-written the scene half a dozen times before delivering) and it is in your interests to make the script as good as possible. You have to believe in yourself ...

Timing

Each draft of your script will be timed. You will be asked to either add or lose time. Some of these potential changes will be suggested to you by the script editor. Experience should enable you to deliver within a minute two either way. Earlier in my career, on different programmes, I heard of one writer delivering nine minutes over and another ten minutes under. They didn't last long. Writing to time is part of being a professional writer, so if you have to read your script out loud, do it.

Research

If your script contains a story about, for instance, adoption, the researcher will read it and if she is not sure about a particular detail, she will check it with her contact. (Researchers build up a network of contacts in various fields). Any changes required will be passed on to you. This is non-negotiable. Your job is to make the research based note fit naturally into the drama and not be dropped in as indigestible exposition. The research should serve the drama, not the other way round.

Typos

We all make them. Any you missed, will be drawn to your attention (It isn't a sacking offence).

Production issues

You may be asked to move a scene from an exterior location to an interior set, or to combine two scenes, cut a scene entirely or lose a character from one or more scenes and possibly add another.

These changes are usually related to the production schedule, and there is basically, nothing you can do about them.

While the script editor is giving you notes, you need to be jotting them down in a way that makes sense to you. I use the hard copy of my first draft and a pencil. It works for me. Don't be afraid to ask the script editor to repeat a note if you're not sure about something and you can always ring them in a day or so if you don't understand your own notes. (It happens)

The number of drafts you do will depend on the programme you write for but it is something you have to learn to live with. The director may be involved at the final draft and he or she will have an input, based on the way they intend to shoot the episode.

Drafting and redrafting

Don't whatever you do, delete your first draft. Start a new document for your second and any subsequent drafts. You may, occasionally, be asked to go back to the version of a scene you wrote in draft one and it's much easier to import it from a previous draft. You should also keep episodes on your hard drive and in hard copy form until they are on screen. You may want to keep a hard copy of every episode you write.

Actually undertaking a second draft can be daunting. You will have worked hard on the script you delivered (at least you should have) and you are being asked to tear it apart, sometimes quite significantly, dropping entire scenes, being asked to make a scene funnier, when you think it's the wittiest thing you've ever written, being told you haven't quite nailed a character's voice. But if you want to be a professional writer, you have to do it. Just try and hang on to that self-belief ...

Fighting back

You don't have to be passive during the editing process. You may disagree with the notes you're being given. You may have had a perfectly valid reason for writing the scene the way you have and you may feel the people who have read the scene haven't got it. If that is the case, say so. It's hard to do if you're starting out, but if you feel strongly, you owe it to yourself to say something.

How often you query a note depends on the kind of writer and the kind of person you are. Some writers will accept virtually every note, without demur. Others will challenge more or less everything, going so far as to refuse to make certain changes.

Most writers, I suspect, fall somewhere in between, prepared to challenge when they feel it is justified, but, equally, accepting a note if they feel it is merited and accepting that they can make it better.

You have to find your own way, and develop your own relationships with script editors, most of whom are a pleasure to work with. They are there to help you, and the editing process can be genuinely creative as you find a better way, together.

Never forget, though, that no matter how strongly you may feel, the Series Producer will have the final say, so bear in mind the saying about banging heads and brick walls.

The script will have your name on it. You want it to be as good as possible. You will need to combine stubbornness, with humility.

14

What does it look like in practice?

An overview

This chapter will show you how a script evolves through successive drafts.

It will give some of the reasons why changes are made as the script is made ready to go into production. And if three drafts might seem daunting, I remember Richard Curtis saying that *Four Weddings and A Funeral* went through seventeen! I'm sure he'd feel it was worth it. Let's look at a scene from the episode we've been considering, through three drafts, to help illustrate the points I've been making. This is scene three in episode 5619. Aaron has arrived at a park in Hotten to continue his community payback sentence, following his conviction for assault. He admitted in court that he was gay, explaining that the violence came out denying who he was. However, the trial was covered in the local paper and Aaron is terrified that his sexuality will be common knowledge. Here is how scene three appeared in first draft.

LOC   AARON/WAYNE/GARY DYSON (COMMUNITY SUPERVISION OFFICER)/NS Young Offenders
SC 3 EXT HOTTEN PARK 08:59 DAY

AARON APPROACHES THE COMMUNITY PAYBACK BOYS AND GIRLS CLUSTERED ROUND GARY DYSON. HE FEELS SELF-CONSCIOUS AS HE SEES WAYNE WHISPER SOMETHING TO SMIGGY, AT HIS SIDE. THEY SNIGGER.

GARY DYSON:	(TO AARON) Cutting it a bit fine, aren't you?
AARON :	Bus was late …
GARY DYSON:	Next time get an earlier one. You know the rules. You get here on time, or else.

AARON NODS AN ACKNOWLEDGEMENT.

GARY DYSON: Today, we're going clear this patch of grass and all the borders. I want every last crisp packet and dog end picking up. Understood?

THE OFFENDERS NOD AND GRUNT THEIR ASSENT.

GARY DYSON: Right. Let's get you into groups.

AS GARY LOOKS ROUND, WAYNE SNEERS AT AARON AND MOVES POINTEDLY AWAY FROM HIM. AARON FEELS WORSE THAN EVER.

CUT TO:

If you look back, you'll see that the scene remains reasonably close to the original story document. I asked in my breakdown if I could give a name to the supervisor and he has become Gary Dyson. I felt it was impossible to tell the scenes at the park (and there are several) without the supervisor having a speaking role. This was accepted.

You'll see too that the group is mixed, boys and girls. This was a question. I raised in my breakdown document and the researcher confirmed that it would be mixed. The job they are doing is clearing a patch of ground, picking up litter etc.

I introduced a non-speaking ally for Wayne, whom I called Smiggy.

Now let's see how the second draft looked:

LOC   AARON/WAYNE/GARY DYSON (COMMUNITY SUPERVISION OFFICER)/ NS Payback Team (2 Boys/2 Girls) SC 3 EXT HOTTEN PARK 08:59 DAY

THE MINIBUS PULLS UP NEXT TO THE LAKE AND THE FENCE, WHICH THE PAYBACK TEAM IS RE-PAINTING. A STORAGE SHED IS CLOSE BY. THE SIX YOUNG OFFENDERS GET OUT OF THE MINIBUS. GARY DYSON, THIRTY - SOMETHING, FIT AND NO-NONSENSE, GETS OUT OF THE DRIVER'S SEAT.

GARY DYSON: Okay guys, listen up. (BEAT) I want you to carry on where you left off yesterday.

		I want four of you painting the fence. Aaron, Wayne, I want you clearing up all the rubbish.
WAYNE	:	Do I have to?
GARY DYSON:		It's not up for discussion. (BEAT) And Aaron: a little reminder. You were nearly late this morning.
AARON	:	It was my bus …
GARY DYSON:		You'd better get an earlier one tomorrow then.
WAYNE	:	Or else you'll get a written warning.
GARY DYSON:		Aaron knows that.
WAYNE	:	Two written warnings, you'll be back in court.
GARY DYSON:		All right, Wayne. (BEAT) Come on. Let's get started …

HE LEADS THE WAY TO THE SHED. WAYNE, A WEASLY BULLY, HANGS BACK WITH AARON, OUT OF GARY'S EARSHOT.

WAYNE	:	So what you here for? You never said yesterday.
AARON	:	What's it to you?
WAYNE	:	Did you nick a kiddie's scooter?
AARON	:	Get stuffed.
WAYNE	:	Robbed an old granny?
AARON	:	I decked a lad, alright?
WAYNE	:	What, you, you puff …

AARON IS ROCKED. HE WONDERS IF WAYNE KNOWS.

AARON	:	You what?
WAYNE	:	Joke. (BEAT) Moron …
GARY DYSON:		Get a move on, you two!

RELIEVED AARON HEADS TO THE SHED WHERE GARY HANDS OUT EQUIPMENT.

CUT TO:

You'll see that a significant number of changes have been made.

The strap line now includes a specific number of young offenders. This is so that casting will know exactly how many extras to employ for this scene.

Instead of Aaron arriving separately by bus, he comes on the minibus with the others. Research indicated that a group like this would be driven to the venue by their Supervision Officer.

You'll see that the opening stage direction is specific about the task the group will undertake, which is different to merely picking up litter. A fence post becomes part of the drama later in the episode. The scene is longer. Smiggy has gone, surplus to requirements. Instead of the conversation being between Gary and Aaron, Wayne chips in with smart remarks. Wayne proves to be Aaron's nemesis later in the episode and it was important to establish him early on.

The detail about Aaron being nearly late remains, but I have added an exchange between Wayne (whom I describe as a weasly bully, in case there was any doubt) and Aaron. He is trying to mock and belittle Aaron, the new boy. He calls him a puff. Aaron recoils, thinking he knows the truth about him, but Wayne makes it clear it was just a generic insult. Aaron is relieved. Puff is not a word that would be usually used. But in expressing homophobia, it was deemed essential to use homophobic language.

The scene is stronger, there is more going on. We get to know Wayne early in the piece and set up the antagonism that will spill over later on.

So now let's consider the third and final draft.

LOC   AARON/WAYNE/GARY DYSON (COMMUNITY SUPERVISION OFFICER)/ NS Payback Team (2 Boys/2 Girls) SC 3 EXT HOTTEN PARK 08:59 DAY

THE MINIBUS PULLS UP NEXT TO THE LAKE AND THE FENCE. A STORAGE SHED IS CLOSE BY. THE SIX YOUNG OFFENDERS GET OUT OF THE MINIBUS. GARY DYSON GETS OUT OF THE DRIVER'S SEAT.

GARY: Okay guys, I want you to carry on where you left off yesterday. (TO WAYNE AND

	AARON) You two, there's a fence needs fixing.
WAYNE:	What? On our own? ...
GARY :	Unless you want me to hold your hand. (BEAT) Aaron: you were late this morning.
AARON:	It was my bus ...
GARY :	Make sure you get an earlier one tomorrow then.
WAYNE:	Or else you'll get a written warning.
GARY :	He (AARON) knows that.
WAYNE:	Two written warnings, you'll be back in court.
GARY :	All right, Wayne. (BEAT) Come on. Let's get started ...

HE LEADS THE WAY TO THE SHED. WAYNE, A WEASLY BULLY, HANGS BACK WITH AARON, OUT OF GARY'S EARSHOT.

WAYNE:	So what you here for? You never said yesterday. Did you nick a kiddie's scooter?
AARON:	Get stuffed.
WAYNE:	Robbed an old granny?
AARON:	I decked a lad, alright?
WAYNE:	What, you, you puff ...

AARON IS ROCKED.

AARON:	You what?
WAYNE:	Joke. (BEAT) Moron ...
GARY :	Get a move on, you two!

RELIEVED AARON HEADS TO THE SHED WHERE GARY HANDS OUT EQUIPMENT.

CUT TO:

You'll notice that there are fewer changes from draft two to this final draft.

The opening stage direction has been changed again. The detail about the payback team re-painting has been removed. The director is on-board at this point and he knows what they'll be doing. Similarly, the thumbnail description of Gary has gone. Casting wanted a freer hand in finding someone.

Gary's first speech now points Aaron and Wayne to the work on the fence. Having looked at the script, the director decided that instead of Aaron being locked in a shed, he wanted Wayne to trip Aaron up with the fence post and have him fall into the lake, getting soaked. And he was right; it was a much more dramatic, visual image than being locked in a shed.

The next two speeches change, becoming a bit more characterful.

There are then two minor tweaks in the ensuing dialogue. Gary says "He" rather than "Aaron", a tiny detail, but it was felt to be more natural.

And two of Wayne's speeches have been run together, to save a few seconds. At the very final stage of the editing process, it can be about finding the tiniest of trims.

So, you'll see, in this instance, the edits were not too painful or indeed onerous. They involved changing stage directions, adding some dialogue by giving it to a character that was silent in the first draft and dropping a superfluous non-speaking character. In every instance, the changes were for the good of the script. Although they are both temporary characters, Wayne is more important than Gary, so it is right that we hear him; the change of activity undertaken by the group leads to a more successful scene later in the episode.

If you do become a professional writer, on a Soap, or elsewhere, be prepared for the editing process. Some will be a lot more severe and challenging than the one above, some less so.

It's very difficult to edit your own work. A fresh pair of eyes can find things you may have missed. Try to remain positive.

15 Make yourself invaluable

An overview

This chapter will look at life beyond the trial script and beyond the first commission and consider how to sustain a career as a Soap writer.

You've arrived on a Soap. You are part of the team; you have delivered for first commissioned episode; you have survived your first edit. Some writers stay on Soaps for many years. They contribute scripts of the right quality, they understand the programme, they know which stories work and which don't. They have gained the respect of their fellow writers, of directors and actors. In other words, they have made themselves invaluable. How do you build on your initial breakthrough and become an established writer?

It's the writing, stupid

No matter how vociferous you are around the conference table, no matter how many stories you pitch, it is the quality of your writing that will determine your future on the show. So, don't assume you are the finished article when you arrive. You will be working with some very experienced people, writers, producers and script editors. So be prepared to listen and learn. Like any skill, writing is something that can be honed and refined. No writer worth his or her salt is ever going to admit they have all the answers. They will be constantly looking for ways to improve, for new ways of expressing their ideas and the same applies to the newly arrived Soap writers.

Pay attention to what the script editors say. They will have been doing the job a lot longer than you and will have worked with a lot of writers. They will be scrupulously professional and won't tell you to "write like so and so" … but they may point you in the direction of a writer who has a take on a particular character and send you a couple of scenes to look at.

You may be sent DVDs of every episode; you may get to look at hard copies of other writers' scripts, but if you don't, make sure you watch the programme, and try not to miss one, and don't forget the online players that TV stations have; a great way for a writer to keep up to date. Look at the way your fellow writers structure their episodes, the way they handle dialogue and shape individual scenes. You will be impressed by some, no doubt, and feel a little unworthy, but in other cases, you will feel that you are every bit as good as your colleague. And the chances are, you will be. So look for ways to improve. Don't argue with notes for the sake of it; see them as an opportunity to make yourself a better writer.

Coming up with the killer story

This book has had a lot to say about story, and for a very good reason. If you can come up with a story that has the legs to play over months rather than weeks, to involve some of the key members of the cast and to affect the lives of others, then it will be noticed. Although, once pitched, the story becomes common property, you should contribute throughout its life on the show, helping to steer it, finding new twists and turns. It will be remembered and spoken of as your story and it will do your standing in the show no harm at all.

Finding the immortal character

Some families and individual characters emerge from discussion round the table, but from time to time you will have the opportunity to pitch a new character in the way that you might pitch a new story. I can look at several characters in *Emmerdale* and pinpoint the moment of their conception, and recall the writer who came up with them.

You need to be as detailed as you can. You will have identified a space for them in the show, so go ahead and create them, as if they were a character in one of your own, original pieces. Give them a name, say where they come from, how old they are, what job they do, what their family background is and who they might be involved with. Give them the Back Story we discussed earlier.

Give an idea of the sort of personality they have and make clear where they might fit in the show. Where will they live and work? Who will they get on with, who won't they like? Who might they fall in love with? What might be their impact on the community? Give them an In-story, a way of getting them in that has a story attached to it.

The chances are, that they character will evolve, and move beyond your original pitch. But that doesn't matter. You gave birth to them. They're your baby.

Team players ... and the awkward squad

I have been fortunate to work for most of my life as a Soap writer, with generally supportive and friendly groups of fellow writers. But that isn't always the case. Writers come in all shapes and sizes, temperament wise and some don't enjoy the collective nature of the programmes as much as others. You will inevitably come across writers who aren't especially friendly, who may dismiss your ideas with a one line put down and who will make it clear that you are very much the new girl or boy.

You may recognise that type, you might be that type yourself, but if not, you have to learn how to cope with that situation. And. let's face it, you could encounter the same dynamics in an office, a school staff room or on the factory floor. The most awkward member of the group might also be the best and most experienced writer, so they're not going anywhere. You have to try and gain their respect, by the quality of your contributions and the quality of your scripts.

I like to think that by nature I am a team player and not prone to putting people down, but I do talk a lot round the table and less experienced writers might find that off putting and intimidating. You will have to find your own way. It is possible to sit in virtual silence throughout a script conference and survive for a long time, but you miss out on so many opportunities. Of course, if you work on a show that doesn't have conferences, this won't be a problem, but you need to be prepared.

New horizons

You may be blessed with skills not shared by some of your fellow writers. Soaps are increasingly looking to have an on-line presence. This involves writing extra scenes, built around scenes that will appear on TV in the regular slots.

So, for instance, you may watch a girl splitting up with her boyfriend as you watch the evening's episode. But you may then be able to go to your computer or your mobile phone and find out what happened before and after what you have watched. The scenes will be written by a member of the writing team and it may offer you an additional chance to shine.

You're only as good as your last script

No matter how experienced you are, you should never take your job on a Soap for granted. If you become complacent, then the quality of your work will almost certainly dip and you may find your star waning rapidly. You may feel that your current producer values you and would never fire you, but producers don't stay on Soaps forever, the job is too stressful. So when a new producer arrives, you have to prove yourself all over again. Many producers arrive and look to shake up the writing team. They may have a couple of writers in mind, ones they've worked with before, and be looking to find them a place on the show. And that often means someone has to go. So you need to be on your mettle. And, be honest, if you become lazy and complacent and deliver substandard scripts, you'll get what you deserve.

Is there life beyond Soap?

It might seem like a daft question since the point of this book is to help you become a Soap writer. But, in a word, the answer is yes, there is.

No matter how brief your stay on a Soap, unless it is a complete disaster, you will learn valuable, marketable skills. Producers are always looking for writers with talent and originality and if you make an impression, you will be remembered. Today's storyline writer or script editor may be tomorrow's producer and if you stay in the business long enough, you will come across the same names and faces throughout your career.

So, if life on one Soap doesn't work out, you can always look to another. You may want to try and move to one of the prime time hour long dramas, like *Casualty* or *Holby City*, which will present a different set of challenges.

You may want to see your own authored work on TV. If you work on Soap, you will meet people who will be able to help you achieve that ambition some time. It is difficult, but not impossible and proving yourself on a Soap is going to stand you in good stead. You will probably want to try and develop your own, individual projects while working on a Soap. Many writers do. And. as a freelance, you are fully entitled to do so. However, you have to be careful not to short change the Soap. That is the programme which provides you with a regular income and you have to demonstrate a level of commitment, or you're not much use to them. There may be occasions when you ask not to be commissioned for a few months in order to complete another project, or you may prefer to work seven days a week, round the clock and try and do both.

You may not have to do anything to plan your next move. You may be invited to contribute to another programme or to submit a pilot episode for a new show, by someone who has seen and enjoyed your work.

So, other doors may open, without you having to push.

A lot depends on how you see yourself. I said at the beginning of the book that some writers come to Soap after a career in other TV drama, or stage and radio drama. Others begin their careers in Soap. Whichever route brings you to Soap, do not listen to those who say writing for one of those wonderful programmes is somehow a lesser skill, because it isn't. It takes dedication, skill and commitment. I am enormously proud of my career, and the fact that I've spent a large part of my working life bringing quality drama to millions of people. I hope that one day you get the opportunity to find out what that feels like.

16 And finally ...

An overview

You are about to see the storyline document for episode 5620, which followed immediately after the one we have looked at throughout the book, episode 5619.

This is the chance to put into practice all the skills you have learned, step-by-step.

So, first, write a scene-by-scene breakdown for the episode, in the manner show earlier. This process may not be required for each Soap, but it is an excellent way to learn about shape and structure and the movement of stories throughout an episode.

When you work on a programme, you will be given details of which spaces are studio sets and which are location. Don't worry too much about that in this exercise; concentrate on the shape of the drama and the interaction of the characters.

When you have completed the breakdown, write the script. Using all the lessons you have learned about dialogue, the shape of scenes, the need for a strong end of part one and end of episode hook, make it as vivid and original as you can.

Episode 5620 Prod: 4/4 Unit 1
WRITER: Chris Thompson

RECORDING:	12th–23rd April 2010
TRANSMISSION:	Thurs 27th May 2010

TX SUNRISE:	0448	VTR SUNRISE:	0602
TX SUNSET:	2120	VTR SUNSET:	2011

Darkness is half an hour before sunrise and half an hour after sunset.

EDNA BIRCH	IN	JOHN BARTON	IN
EVE BIRCH	IN	MOIRA BARTON	
RODNEY BLACKSTOCK		HOLLY BARTON	
ZAK DINGLE		ADAM BARTON	IN
SAM DINGLE		NICOLA DE SOUZA	IN
CAIN DINGLE		LEYLA HARDING	IN
DEBBIE DINGLE		PEARL LADDERBANKS	
CHAS DINGLE		LIZZIE LAKELY	
MARLON DINGLE		FAYE LAMB	IN
BETTY EAGLETON		RYAN LAMB	
BOB HOPE	IN	AARON LIVESY	IN
VIV HOPE	IN	DAVID METCALFE	IN
CARL KING		DOUGLAS POTTS	IN
JIMMY KING		BRENDA WALKER	
PADDY KIRK	IN	GENNIE WALKER	
VAL LAMBERT		DANNY	IN
ERIC POLLARD		WAYNE	IN
NIKHIL SHARMA		SCARLETT NICHOLS	IN
JAI SHARMA	IN	**JUVENILES**	
ANDY SUGDEN	IN	HANNAH BARTON	IN
DIANE SUGDEN	IN	BELLE DINGLE	
KATIE SUGDEN		SAMSON DINGLE	
CHARITY TATE		ANGELICA KING	
ASHLEY THOMAS		ARTHUR THOMAS	
LAUREL THOMAS		CATHY HOPE	
ALAN TURNER		HEATH HOPE	
TERRY WOODS	IN	SARAH SUGDEN	
NATASHA WYLDE	IN	VICTORIA SUGDEN	IN
MAISIE WYLDE		GABRIELLE THOMAS	
NATHAN WYLDE	IN	NOAH TATE	
CHARLIE	IN	TJ WOODS	
DECLAN	IN	WILL WYLDE	
JACKSON	IN	**ADDITIONAL CAST**	
TOTAL CHARACTERS	25	**TOTAL JUVENILES**	2

- **Aaron feels more isolated than ever**.
- Natasha's growing weary of Nathan's loathing of Declan.
- The Barton's have no sympathy for Holly.

Hook: Aaron realises he's no chance with Jackson.

Thursday 27th May (Continuous)

A) Aaron

P/U: Aaron's locked in the shed by homophobic Wayne.

With laughter ringing in his ears, **AARON** kicks he door of the shed and barks at the lads to open up. Hearing the laughter subside, Aaron sees the door open and **DANNY**, his probation officer wonders if he's okay. Humiliated, Aaron covers that he is fine. Grimly heading out past a smirking **WAYNE,** Aaron can't even find the words to have a go; he just wants to get out of there.

With **SCARLETT, ADAM** clocks Aaron heading home and wonders if they're still on for tonight. Brooding, Aaron snaps he's not in the mood. Scarlett looks glad to have Adam to herself until Aaron boils over. Letting rip, Aaron admits the homophobic idiots locked him in the shed and he didn't even stop long enough to punch them. Adam's saddened as Aaron reckons this is exactly everything he had feared would happen if he came out. Wanting to support his mate, Adam claims that is all the more reason to go out tonight and forget the lot of them. Despite himself, Aaron smiles.

Aaron is upstairs when Adam arrives at Smithy and **PADDY** quietly notes he seemed a bit down when he got in. Adam reckons Aaron's had a tough day and Paddy's about to inquire further when they hear Aaron approaching. Lightening the tone, Paddy winds up Adam about his strong aftershave, laughing it might get him some attention. Aaron relaxes to hear Adam getting a hard time.

Outside the club, Adam senses Aaron has quietened. Genuinely a bit intimidated, Adam hopes Aaron is going to look out for him. Aware he's struggling himself to do this, Aaron gruffly teases he'll hold his hand. Steeling themselves, the lads walk into the bar.

In the bar, Aaron manages to relax a little as Adam jokes he's never felt so popular. Clocking a guy looking over, Adam reckons Aaron has an admirer. As the guy heads across and makes a beeline for Adam, Aaron is amused to see his mate like a rabbit in the headlights.

Seeing Adam fending off the guy's advances, Aaron nobly steps in and suggests the pair of them are already attached. As the guy backs off, Aaron ribs Adam for being so tongue-tied. Seeing the funny side, Adam finally laughs. Glancing through the crowd, Aaron catches the stony glare of **JACKSON** and falters.

Jackson tears into Aaron for daring to come back after what he did. Aware Jackson's drawing attention to him, Aaron urges him to see he's sorry. Adam defends his mate, insisting Jackson knows Aaron was going through a rough time. Dismissive, Jackson reckons loads of blokes have been through the same but they didn't turn into psychos. Aaron appeals to Jackson to remember how good they were together. Dismissive, Jackson reckons that was before Aaron showed his true colours. Aaron is cut.

Going after Jackson, Aaron tries to convince him he isn't like that and hints at the homophobic nightmare he's suffered at community service that morning. Cold, Jackson spells it out to Aaron—gay or straight he's a thug and his type isn't welcome there. Seeing Aaron's utter humiliation as people turn and stare, Adam urges him to leave. Aaron reluctantly allows Adam usher him out.

Outside the bar, Aaron refuses to go home, insisting he needs to try and make Jackson see the truth about him. Feeling for his mate, Adam nods Aaron in the direction of the bar, and he turns to see Jackson kissing another man. Aaron's gutted to see Jackson is totally over him, he's ruined his chances for good with the only person who ever truly understood what he is going through.

B) Home farm

P/U: Declan admits that his attraction to Natasha is very real.

At Home Farm, **EDNA** and **EVE** have called to discuss **NICOLA**'s wedding flowers and how to decorate Home farm for the reception. As the women argue, **DECLAN** orders Nicola to take her wedding stress elsewhere, before going back to the phone to give a planning officer hell. Nicola apologises but there's a sense it isn't just the wedding fraying her nerves. (*Impending court case.*) Off the phone, Declan berates the small minded idiots and their power games. **NATASHA** laughs she's glad she wasn't on the other end of the phone. There's a real growing chemistry as the normally unflappable Natasha is unable to hold Declan's gaze.

In the Home Farm shop with **DOUG, LEYLA** is talking to **DAVID** about their future plans, or lack of them when Declan arrives in with Nathan. Getting David aside, Declan wonders if all council people are so short sighted and asks if he is more enterprising and would be interested in cutting a deal. Paranoid (re: his own minor corruption), David reckons they have procedures to follow. As **NATHAN** tells Leyla he needs her to send stock back before the shop closes, Doug is pained to see Leyla unable to stop the shop closure despite having ideas to take it on.

Leyla has final stab at pushing thoughts she's had for rejuvenating the shop and keeping her job. Loyal Doug urges Declan to take Leyla seriously. Declan tells Leyla it's a done deal but is sure her ideas are viable and casually suggests she put together a little business plan for herself. Leyla is frustrated that she hasn't got the funds. Nathan advises Leyla to stick to being a shop girl.

Natasha's 'keep things professional' stance is beginning to waver as Declan emerges looking gorgeous ready for the business do with Jai. When Declan invites her along, Natasha declines. Casually explaining her and Nikhil are off to see a film, as mates, Maisie urges her mum to go and Declan flashes a tempting smile. Natasha relents, needing time to get ready. Glad, Declan is sure Natasha is worth waiting for. Natasha feels a frisson of excitement.

Natasha and Declan head into the pub to meet **JAI** and see **FAYE** is there too, chatting closely with Jai. As Natasha and Faye realise they are going out together, there is an obvious moment of tension. Aside, Declan assures Natasha he had no idea Faye was coming. Refusing to let it spoil things, Faye and Natasha exchange uneasy smiles, aware they're both moving with life.

Arriving back at Home Farm having had a good time, Natasha finds Nathan slumped in front of the TV. Glad she's finally decided to come home, Nathan explains Will was up earlier but he saw to him for her. Natasha's grateful but sharply asks if Nathan has been waiting up to check on her. Denying, Nathan admits he is glad to see she's come home alone at least. Growing weary of Nathan's remarks, Natasha tells Nathan she's going to bed.

C) Charlie & Diane

P/U: *Diane's had the time of her life with Charlie in Paris.*

DIANE sees **CHARLIE** talking on his mobile. As Charlie ends the call, he questions Diane's amused expression. Diane admits he sounds so … *French*. Dry, **VICTORIA** reckons that's the point; he's speaking French. Thanking Victoria for her support, Charlie lightly confides that he's going to have to go back to France to oversee the final house renovations. Diane reckons he's a lucky man, but it's clear she's uneasily struck by Charlie's throwaway comment about France being like home to him.

Polishing the shop window, concerned Leyla confides in Doug about what's going on with Bob and Gennie. Clocking Diane passing, Doug notes things must be getting serious between her and Charlie if he's whisking her away for weekends in Paris. Uneasy, Diane again apologises to Doug, asserting she doesn't want lose his friendship. When Doug genuinely admits he never wanted that either, a guilty Diane implies she's not even sure how much longer Charlie will be sticking around. Doug tries to hide it, but Leyla notes he's gladdened Charlie might not be here to stay.

Charlie informs Diane he's going over to France next week and invites her to make a holiday of it. Seeing Diane's hesitation, Charlie assures Victoria could come too—sure she'd be back in time for her last exam. Guarding against her growing feelings, Diane questions if they're moving too fast, neither knows where this is leading. Charlie wonders if that's such a bad thing; it's called adventure. Throwing caution to the wind, Diane's sold.

D) Viv, Bob & Gennie

P/U: Bob vows to fight for his kids.

VIV sees **BOB** on the doorstep of Connelton chatting to **TERRY** and tersely informs him she has been to the solicitors. Irritated, Viv agrees Bob can have keys to the shop and café but he can't set foot in the flat. Bob begs Viv to discuss seeing the kids but she coldly retorts her solicitor has said her prison sentence will not affect her claim for custody. Bob boils.

Bob vents to Terry at how unreasonable Viv is being. Bob insists tried to make it right but Terry cautiously reckons he can't blame Viv for acting like this, she is his wife, they have children together and Bob slept with Gennie while she was in prison. However Bob spins it, those are the facts. Bob doesn't need reminding.

Viv's locking the shop up when Bob appears and insists he can't believe they have come to this. At breaking point, Bob wants to see his kids and he pushes past her to get up to flat (Betty's babysitting). Viv bars his way and swears if he defies her wishes she'll use it all in court. Bob backs down, not taking the threat idly and pleads they might be over, but the kids need both their parents. Wavering, Viv agrees Bob can have minimal contact until it's officially sorted. Bob will take whatever scraps Viv offers.

E) Holly & the Bartons

P/U: Hannah's guilty to know she kept Holly's secret for so long.

In the yard, **JOHN** tells Adam and **ANDY** it's time for a break and calls for Holly, who is doing menial work in the barn. Seeing John despairing at Holly's self-pity routine as she fails to respond, Andy wonders if everything is okay. Stressed out, John explains about Holly, the drugs and how he and Moira have differing views about how to deal with this. Andy guesses it's causing a lot of strain and John nods, just hoping he's getting it right.

Back from school, **HANNAH** finds John and claims she's got something to confess. As Andy makes a diplomatic exit, Hannah admits she knew a while ago Holly had been kicked out of college, but didn't know why. Dry, John guesses Holly persuaded her to keep quiet. Confirming, Hannah worries she has inadvertently enabled Holly to take drugs. John assures Hannah that Holly has to take responsibly for herself and is riled at how sneaky Holly's been.

As you embark on this exercise, you should know as much about writing Soap as there is to know. Well, as much as I know, anyway. The rest is up to you.

Good luck.

Index